How to Grow a Women's Minis-Tree

Harvesting the Power of God's Woman

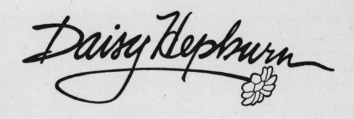

Daisy Hepburn

GL
Regal Books

Published by Regal Books
A Division of GL Publications
Ventura, California 93006
Printed in U.S.A.

Library of Congress Cataloging in Publication Data

Hepburn, Daisy.
    How to grow a women's minis-tree.

    Bibliography: p.
    1. Women in church work. 2. Women—Religious life.
I. Klope, Joan Bay, 1959-   .   II. Title.
BV4415.H45   1986   253'.088042   86-11812
ISBN 0-8307-1159-7

2 3 4 5 6 7 8 9 10 / 91 90 89 88

Rights for publishing this book in other languages are contracted by Gospel Literature International (GLINT) foundation. GLINT also provides technical help for the adaptation, translation, and publishing of Bible study resources and books in scores of languages worldwide. For further information, contact GLINT, Post Office Box 488, Rosemead, California, 91770, U.S.A., or the publisher.

Oh, the joys of those who do not follow evil men's advice, who do not hang around with sinners, scoffing at the things of God: But they delight in doing everything God wants them to, and day and night are always meditating on his laws and thinking about ways to follow him more closely.

They are like trees along a river bank bearing luscious fruit each season without fail. Their leaves shall never wither, and all they do shall prosper.

(Ps. 1:1-3, TLB)

Dedication

To David on the occasion of our
thirty-fifth anniversary with my love.

And to our children
Lois, David and Carol.

"For this God is our God
for ever and ever;
he will be our guide even
to the end" (Ps. 48:14, *NIV*).

Contents

Acknowledgments

Someone has defined a ministry as any relationship in which both parties benefit. I do believe it is true. And I gratefully acknowledge those who have benefited me as I have visited their churches across our country. The principles in this book have been developed through years of observing how deeply God's women desire a more fruitful, vital and growing church ministry.

Just as we have shared these steps to growing a women's ministry in seminars and conferences, there have also been many special women who have served with me on committees. Their creativity, cheerful service, hospitality and diligence to detail have made these times both charming and productive. Can I count on God to reward their efforts? Yes! But I humbly acknowledge their ministry.

Often I am asked about my family. David and I are "empty nesting" now and I thank him for his unfailing love, support and blessing on what God has given me to do. Without it I would be neither willing nor able to fulfill my assignment.

Joan Bay Klope is an editor, younger sister in the Lord, mother-to-be and prayer partner whose writing skills and dedication to this task has truly made it possible. I am very grateful.

Can I say that this book is much needed material for women in churches? It is my prayer that it will encourage and enable women to serve the Lord with gladness, knowing full well that it is God who makes things grow (see 1 Cor. 3:7, *TLB*).

1
Examining
Our Roots

When I consider my own roots, several incredible women come to mind—women who were faithful servants and valuable role models. But my grandma was an exceptional model for ministry. At the turn of the century she and Grandpa left their native England to serve as missionaries in the Texas oil fields. Grandma's zeal for reaching others was born one afternoon at the age of 12 when she was converted at a storefront Salvation Army meeting.

The areas of service Grandma envisioned were unlimited and everything she touched was enlivened with opportunities for the Lord Jesus. Street-corner meetings, fellowship gatherings for women, camps for children, Saturday afternoon visitations—even adopting several children who were homeless—all of these acts of service were an everyday part of her life.

Grandma was also a prayer warrior and I remember believing that the windows of heaven would actually open up and pour out the answers to her prayers—right on the spot! She was a powerful, short and gifted servant of God.

But how did Grandma learn to serve so effectively? After all, there were no ministry tools available to her. Besides her burning desire to serve the Lord and a gift of creativity, Grandma simply did what she felt had to be done. She planted the seeds, cultivated the limited resources around her and depended on God "who makes things grow" (1 Cor. 3:7, *TLB*).

Wanting to Serve

I've observed the same deep-rooted desire to faithfully serve the Lord many times since as I travel across the country.

• It's certainly present in the women of Santa Clara County, California. How beautifully they are responding to the growing Asian and Hispanic populations in their communities by providing numerous ministries to meet the growing spiritual and cultural needs.

• Meet Anita, an Air Force Chaplain's wife who pours herself into the lives of the servicemen's wives around her. So many are desperately alone and feel uprooted as they travel around the world. Anita offers stable and consistent friendships to these women on whatever base she and her husband serve.

• Esther is a woman who has a special place in her heart for the older widows and single women in her church. Once a month, after the Sunday service, she gathers this great group together and they lunch at a local restaurant. She reports that the fellowship is unsurpassed and I believe her. On the Sunday that I joined the group there were 44 in attendance!

• Lucille lives in Minnesota and recently sponsored a Valentine drop-in celebration in her home. Besides enjoying delicious homemade goodies and freshly brewed coffee, the women brought canned goods and clothes and made love gifts for a family in desperate need of the everyday essentials. Unemployment was taking its toll in their lives and Lucille and her 35 friends did something about it while enjoying the holiday.

Not only are these women touching lives for Jesus, but their personal desires to serve the Lord are being met. Amid the national trends to get color coordinated and self-actualized, many Christian women are making it clear that *service* is a high priority in their lives. Does this surprise you?

This unique and beautiful fact became especially clear to me one afternoon as I perused the newsstands at the O'Hare International Airport in Chicago. It was the Sunday edition the publishers were trying to sell and the editors of the *Chicago Sun Times* did an excellent job of getting my attention. It read quite simply, "What Women Want." With pen in hand and interest stirred, I wrote down the three "greatest" desires of modern American women:

1. More sexual freedom
2. A bigger role at work
3. More help at home.

How our motivations as Christian women differ from our secular sisters! We are deeply committed to Jesus Christ and have far greater reasons for laying our petitions before the Lord each morning:

"Lord, I want to serve you."
"Lord, I want you to receive glory from my life."
"Heavenly Father, may you be Lord in every avenue of my life."

Let's not let the media sell us short! We are a group of women who want things far more significant. We care about women who are raising their children alone or who are suffering from personal tragedy. We want to live bravely and serve others so the needs around us can be met.

The Best Job Around

The cover photo of the first 1983 issue of *Time* magazine shows a missionary preaching the gospel in New Guinea. Inside various missionary organizations highlight their foreign mission goals for the decade of the '80s.

Timothy Wyma, a missionary serving the jungles of Bolivia under New Tribes Missions explains, "To me, this is the only job in the world that is big enough. If you are looking for something that needs all you have, this is it."[1]

What is your attitude when serving on the mission fields located in your own backyard?

But we have needs too, don't we? When examining our roots we must consider our wants as well as our needs, for both go hand in hand. Sometimes our burning desires to serve are squelched by fears.

We Need to Grow Up

Some of us have made it our life's work to attend Bible studies. Scripture says in 2 Timothy 3 that the study of the Word of God is not an end in itself. To simply feel super spiritual because we have spent 15 or 20 years in Bible study is not adequate as I understand it. The Word of God is designed to equip us to work.

> *But you must keep on believing the things you have been taught. You know they are true for you know that you can trust those of us who have taught you. You know how, when you were a small child, you were taught the holy Scriptures; and it is these that make you wise to accept God's salvation by trusting in Christ Jesus. The whole Bible was given to us by inspiration from God and is useful to teach us what is true and to make us realize what is wrong in our lives; it straightens us out and helps us to do what is right. It is God's way of making us well prepared at every point, fully equipped to do good to everyone.*
> *(2 Tim. 3:14-17, TLB)*

Take a moment and consider the women's ministry

programs at your church. No doubt you have heard these and other stunting comments from time to time:

> "Personally, I don't have time for endless reading of the minutes and treasurer's reports."

> "My personal priorities do not include getting together with the little old ladies for tea and crumpets."

> "Until it's good enough, I'll not involve myself."

> "I've decided to go back to school. I need a challenge to my mind and intelligence because I'm getting rusty."

As if these attitudes are not damaging enough, still others fear that growth will never be possible because the number of you is too small, your facilities too cramped or the focus of the program too narrow. Perhaps it is time we break up our holy huddles and challenge ourselves to act upon our biblical training. Let's grow up. Our great big God is waiting!

We Need a Clearer Perspective of God

I have a special friend who is retired from serving the Lord on the mission field in Alaska, but currently serves as a children's worker in a church on the West Coast. Her name is Louise Matson and she has had a tremendous impact on my life and the lives of others. Over 50 years ago she and her Mennonite family escaped from Russia. And God bless her, she has faithfully served the Lord in incredible ways ever since.

At a particular church gathering several years ago Aunt Louise (as many of us so fondly refer to her) gave each of the children in attendance a piece of burlap, some glue, a pair of scissors and other scraps of material. She then asked them to make a banner. When they were all finished she ran around and looked carefully at their creations. After examining one particular banner (which she has since given to me) she asked the little boy who had made it, "Brian, what does your banner say?"

"It says," he eagerly replied, "God is good."

Aunt Louise gently but firmly said, "You know what, Brian? It might have been better if you could have gotten it all on the front of the banner. That way people would have been able to read what it says."

"I know, Aunt Louise," Brian said, "but my God is too big!"

If only we had that problem! Most of us find ourselves serving a God who just about fits onto our banners. What we need to do is realize that we serve a God who is bigger than pumpkin bars and coffee. He cares about the fact that a good deal of the basin and towel service available at our churches is accomplished by us. But for those of us who see that God has given us a delightful opportunity as well as a heavy responsibility, He will draw close and give us great visions. Imagine the experiences we will miss if we choose NOT to cooperate with the Lord.

We Need Courage

Stop for a moment and read Romans 15. Rediscover God's marvelous truth and apply it to the women's ministry program you are involved in. As we move in and out of each other's lives, meeting needs, opening ourselves up and loving each other because of our commonality to Jesus Christ, God will get the glory. What do we need? *Courage*—received from our personal reserves and from those women who daily offer us encouragement.

Let us dare to take that little prefix from the word *encouragement* and think about it. What does the prefix "en" mean? Loosely translated it means, "to make possible." Enable. Enact. Something you bring into being. Encouragement therefore involves helping someone. Being brave. Moving out and beyond our normal scope of activities. As Christian women we're not interested in competing—we're interested in the courageous activity of growing a women's ministry and encouraging one another. We need courage and we can get it from the Lord and from each other.

We Need Enabling

Perhaps the greatest problem in our churches today is this: *We have been overchallenged and under-enabled.* Across America I have heard these frustrations expressed time and time again.

• "I've read about Release Time Programs in other states and because my children are in public school, I'm interested in seeing this program made available here. But how do I organize such a move?"

• "I'm disgusted that an adult video shop has opened up just two blocks away from our neighborhood, but what do I do? I'm not the picketing type. Who will listen, anyway?"

• "I really do care about those in prison. I think quite often about them—especially during the holidays. But I don't know what I can do. I can't just walk up and say 'Here I am.'"

• "We have many farm workers coming and going throughout our community as they follow the crops. They need to hear the Good News but many don't speak English. A reading clinic would be such a great program but I don't know how to get one started."

It is for these reasons and more that I'm excited

about sharing with you some enabling techniques I've learned and developed. Growing a women's ministry is exciting and I understand your need for enabling skills. Come with me and we'll design a program together. The pattern is so versatile that you will be able to apply it to whatever church organization you are involved in. And best of all, when we are finished, the Lord Jesus will be getting the glory! Let's begin an unprecedented adventure with Him!

Pray with me, won't you?

Heavenly Father,
You know of our deep-rooted desire to serve. You are also aware of our needs—to grow up, to clarify your perspective on ministry and to gain courage and enabling skills. Forgive us for our stunting attitudes and our lack of faith. Fill us, instead, with your character—and may it be revealed in our lives. May those that we meet and greet everyday be caused to wonder about our motivation. Thank you for giving us this opportunity to examine our roots. In Christ's precious name we pray. Amen.

This is what
the Sovereign LORD says:

*I myself will take a shoot from the very top
of a cedar and plant it;
I will break off a tender sprig from its
topmost shoots and plant it
on a high and lofty mountain.
On the mountain heights of Israel I will
plant it;
it will produce branches and bear fruit and
become a splendid cedar.
Birds of every kind will nest in it;
they will find shelter in the shade of its
branches.
All the trees of the field will know that
I the* LORD *bring down the tall tree
and make the low tree grow tall.
I dry up the green tree and make the
dry tree flourish . . . I WILL DO IT.*

(Ezek. 17:22-24, NIV)

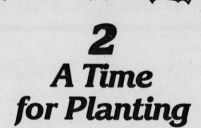

2
A Time
for Planting

It is wonderful having a deeply-rooted desire to serve, isn't it! And I can't think of a better time to begin planting than now. Goodness knows there are plenty of fertile fields awaiting among the women in our lives. But just as a farmer doesn't haphazardly throw any 'ol seed onto a plowed field, so must we avoid the temptation to make programs available simply because they sound good or are easily organized. *We must learn how to accurately assess the needs in our churches and communities.* It will *then* be possible for us to design fruitful ministries to meet those needs.

Avoid the Great Ministry Pitfall

One of the greatest pitfalls of ministry is to choose the path of least resistance by hiring a speaker, sending out publicity and event notices, arranging for some special music and gathering a crowd. Depending upon the size of the response you no doubt will feel that your ministry, as a whole, is a success or a failure.

But above and beyond this immediate experience, this kind of approach to ministry excludes the opportunity of ever *really* coming to grips with the specific needs women have in your community. Putting on a program and *hoping* someone will come or giving women the opportunity to hear yet another speaker is missing the mark. It is a far more productive ministry that (1) catches sight of what the real needs of the women are and (2) plans programs that really touch and affect lives. May we stop congregating people who will meet anonymously and come away with information that they find "interesting" or "thought-provoking." The Lord Jesus calls us to be life-changers!

Stop for a moment and evaluate your program methodology. Are you avoiding the great ministry pitfall? Perhaps you're wondering just how to go about assessing needs. This is a great place to be because you are now on your way!

Analyzing the Soil

Taking a Profile

"Please take the card in front of you and list how our church ministers to the needs of its people—especially to the women." These instructions were given to a fellowship group I was about to address. Then, almost as an afterthought, the leader asked the women to turn their cards over and list some of the areas where they were personally hurting. I was awfully anxious to see if their results would parallel the discoveries made by churches I have been observing for years. And sure enough, *for them,* a surprising discovery was made: Most members found that the two lists did not correspond at all! Their church's activities and their personal needs were apparently miles apart.

Often—in our best moments—we feel good when our meetings are well attended, finances are in the black, missionaries are being written to, conflict between members is minimal and new programs are being introduced. However, these outward signs of effectiveness do not necessarily mean that the picture is as rosy as it might appear. Our dear women found this to be a personal reality. Developing programs based on "guessti-

mates" is inadequate. I became so interested in identify-
ing felt needs within the Church that I first approached
my own denomination. Although the following list was
compiled from a profile of 2,371 male *and* female members, I found the felt needs fascinating:

1. Desire for instructions in helping non-
   Christians find faith in Jesus Christ.

2. Need for more close friendships with
   those in the church.

3. Perceived need for leading inactive members to a commitment in the life and work
   of the church.

4. Perceived need for more effective training
   programs for teachers and youth workers.

5. Perceived need for resources and materials for developing an ongoing ministry to
   families.

6. Perceived need for a more effective ministry in the immediate church community.

7. Perceived need for effective approach to
   introduce inquirers to life in Christ and
   church membership.

8. Desire for help in learning how to build
   friendships with non-Christians.

9. Perceived need for design in training Sunday School teachers in Bible knowledge.

10. Perceived need for more emphasis on a
    personal prayer life.

11. Perceived need for effective training programs for church officers and leaders.

12. Frequency of Bible study should increase.

The report also noted that 33 percent of those polled rated their women's ministries as being very effective in providing study and fellowship opportunities. Nearly 50 percent gave a "somewhat effective" rating.

At a midweek retreat I asked the women to answer the following questions:

1. What is your age?
2. What is your marital status?
3. What is a need in your life?
4. Is your church meeting that need?
5. What is your own area of ministry?

I received 130 responses (from women whose ages ranged from 23-75) and it was not surprising that the greatest need most often expressed was for a deeper spiritual walk. But along with that—which also meant more disciplined time with the Lord and knowledge of the Word—was the recognition of attitude problems.

"I need to trust the Lord more."
"My need is for patience with my family."
"I need to be more positive and less critical."

At least 25 of the women expressed that their greatest need was for a friend due to loneliness or aloneness. Most of these women were married once. Several expressed a desire to serve the Lord but felt they needed training. Others said they needed to find opportunities to serve because their churches were not providing enabling ministries. Some saw themselves standing at a crossroads, seeking the Lord's guidance for the ministry they felt they should have now that the children were grown and out of the nest. Seventy-three of the 130 I polled indicated that good teaching from the pulpit, small-group Bible studies, support groups and generally good fellowship opportunities met their requirements.

There were many, however, who felt that their needs were misunderstood or ignored. May the following three comments give you some insight into those needs that may go unexpressed:

• "I need guidance regarding divorce in my daughter's life. The church has not been meeting this need and some of the counseling has been detrimental! I lead Bible studies and I'm 49."

• "I need more confidence in myself to do the Lord's work. My church helps by encouraging a little, but I don't think they know that I need at lot of it. I'm 28 years old."

• "I'm a widow and I need friends. We had just moved here when my husband died nine months ago. They have been friendly in church but if *I* had not taken the initiative to get involved (I joined the choir and a Bible study) I would still be alone. I think the church needs to do more on a one-on-one basis. I'm 59 years old."

Aren't these fascinating findings? Taking a profile is an excellent way of testing the soil. But I'd like to introduce four other methods that will provide you with excellent information as well.

Listening Carefully to Your Women

When you have a deep desire to minister effectively, you become sensitive to conversations and to trends. Read magazines, listen to talk shows and take careful note of prayer requests. By keeping your antennae out, you will always be alert to the needs of the women in your sphere of influence. It takes strong personal discipline to be a good listener. So take a close look at your response when someone tells you something and make it your goal to be the kind of woman people want to talk to.

Reading Your Local Newspaper

Set *How to Grow a Women's Minis-Tree* aside for a moment and grab yesterday's newspaper. I have mine right here so we can go through them together. Although you will rarely find anything terribly encouraging or positive, you will be amazed at how needs can be uncovered in this fashion.

For example, the front page of my paper shows a natural disaster—a flood. Over here is a traffic accident report and at the bottom of the page is a court action. Once you become sensitized to needs, you will realize that there are people right here in your community whose names will appear on the pages of your paper. These are the ones in need of your ministry.

Perhaps your paper has an article about a family whose child has been injured in a motorcycle accident. Yet another family may be homeless due to a dwelling fire. Now look at the obituaries. These families are experiencing bereavement. Consider the marriages, divorces and birth announcements. All of these families are experiencing tremendous change. Perhaps there are school activities and various community functions announced on the "people pages." All of these notices compile a genuine list of needs. Take careful note.

Creating a Clever Questionnaire

A fun and cleverly designed questionnaire, given to every woman to fill out, will become an important get-acquainted tool. It will also help the women to discover their own most effective place of ministry.

This method of information-gathering needs to be planned for, because the facts about the women will constantly change. Asking the women to update their sheets once a year is practical and necessary, and you may want them to accomplish this task at the first activity of the year. And yet many women who come and go will no doubt miss the event. To avoid this problem, make the questionnaire available to visitors before every united meeting of women's ministries or *any* meeting where there is the largest number or greatest cross section of the female population in attendance.

Let your creative juices flow as you put together the questionnaire. Some clever artwork, a classy border and an appropriate Bible verse will perk the interest of the women and encourage their serious attention. Here is some of the information you will want to retrieve:

1. Name, address and phone numbers (both home and work)
2. Marital status and number of children (if any)
3. Birth date and age (within a couple of years!)
4. Education and work experiences

5. Hobbies
6. A photo.

There are also a number of questions you will want to ask:

- How did you learn of our women's ministry?
- What areas of ministry are you currently involved in? (Choir, Bible studies, etc.)
- What activities were you involved in last year?
- What kind of ministry programs would benefit you most?
- What suggestions do you have?
- Is there anyone you would like us to invite personally to the next activity?

An actual questionnaire that you are encouraged to photocopy is available in the accompanying resource manual.

A Ministry Hint

Why not create a hospitality booth at your next large gathering of women? Inside set up a photo area and take a Polaroid picture of every new woman in attendance. This can be attached to the questionnaire they have just filled out and posted on a newcomers bulletin board. They will feel so welcome and the regulars will be able to identify guests by name.

Knowing the Scriptural Mandates

Because we are women of God, the ultimate source of information will always come from the revealed Word of God—the Bible. The Scripture is clear—what we are to be doing is NOT optional. Not only does service to others prove our faith but it demonstrates our love for the Lord, and is an act of obedience. Open your Bible to the following four references, reading carefully and meditating on your personal response:

Romans 12:4-12. The apostle Paul says in this passage that each one of us has gifts, according to the grace given to us. List here the seven gifts mentioned:

1.   5.

2.   6.

3.   7.

4.

Paul also talks about loving the members of God's family. In the space provided, list some of the characteristics we should strive to make an essential part of our personalities. And may this list become a personal reminder when you are about to embark on a service project.

James 2:1-10. James tells us that we need to be involved with the people coming into our churches who are unable to carry their share of the financial burdens. List some of the ways your church is acting on this Scripture right now:

Matthew 25:31-46. "When the Son of Man comes in his glory, and all the angels with him, he will sit on his throne in heavenly glory" (Matt. 25:31, *NIV*) and divide the sheep from the goats. What did the sheep do to deserve the Father's blessing?

What did the goats do to deserve their curse?

Remember, Scripture says we are to serve—there is no option. And it is here in this passage that we learn of the seriousness of this command, for those who are capable of serving and choose not to "will go away to eternal punishment" (Matt. 25:46).

Titus 2:3-4. Just consider for a moment what an admonition this is concerning the present problem of alcoholism among the upper middle-class women in our communities! We NEED these women, for they are best suited to train the younger women in the ways of the Lord when they are not under the influence of alcohol. What programs can you think of to help fight alcoholism in your church?

Consider the Women's Society or other group involving the older women in your church. Are you making use of their wisdom and experience? How?

Four additional Scriptures that will be especially helpful to you are James 1:27, Hebrews 13:1-5 and Colossians 3:16; 4:2.

You are now listening carefully to your women, reading local newspapers with a critical eye, extracting information from clever questionnaires and listening with your hearts to the Word of God. Isn't it time to act?

Organizing Your Results

Surprised, are you? I'm sure that you never envisioned the possibilities for ministry you are seeing now. Before these visions become lost in the excitement of the moment, let's create a chart. Not only will this get your ideas down on paper but there will be some semblance of order when you're finished.

NOW!

Begin by listing all of the current areas of ministry the women in your church are involved in.

WOW!

Ignoring for just a moment what you have written above, note here what you believe God has in mind for you and the women's ministry program at your church. Let your sanctified imagination soar.

What have you written? Is it really what *God* has in mind? It is His greatest desire that every family be united in Him, that every child have a hope of eternal life and that everyone be ready for His Second Coming! God never thinks in terms of the world's best Bible study, the champion mother-daughter banquet or the most effective retreat. Although these activities can all be the means to God's purposes, the programs and activities are never His primary goal. Besides, don't be tempted to place this kind of information here—the activities list comes later on in this exercise!

I have been known to call this the prisoner-of-war list. After all, do you ever wonder how we get *anything* accomplished for Jesus' sake when there seems to be so much working against us? Make a list of the excuses or situations that are currently making God's plan for your church seem impossible to realize. Here are a few common excuses I've heard:

> "No one has time anymore."
>
> "We don't have enough facilities for effective ministry."
>
> "Everyone works."
>
> "We lack leadership."
>
> "Nobody wants to get involved."

Place your list here:

Is it reasonable to believe that if God has a high and holy purpose for you and the ministry you are involved in, that He would deliberately make it impossible for you to serve Him? Let's dare to cross out those negatives and take a step of faith—a step that moves us into more dynamic areas of ministry!

This is now the time to dream some big dreams. List some ways you can imagine the Lord would lead you to plan programs to better fulfill His purposes. (If you were tempted earlier to list programs, this is the place for you to legitimately do that.)

A Ministry Hint

Over and over again I have heard women speak of their need for *significance.* And oh, how I can relate! To meet this strongly felt need, I suggest that all of your activities show women that they are planned for. For example, name tags should be printed in large letters so a woman's name can be readily seen and she can be addressed by her name. There should also be greeters and hostesses available so each woman in attendance can be welcomed and cared for in a personal manner. I affirm it in my book, *Look, You're a Leader!* that meeting around tables and creating a warm fellowshiping atmosphere will also give women significance. Even the careful planning of decorations will help women sense their specialness. And lastly, take the time to let the women introduce each other and get acquainted around their tables. This is never a waste of time. Significant? They all are, so take the time and show them.

VOW!

Now this is the hard part. This is your commitment to the task, the declaring of your intention, your getting down to business and saying, "I'm at your service, Lord." I encourage you to write a short prayer, dedicating yourself and your dreams to Him.

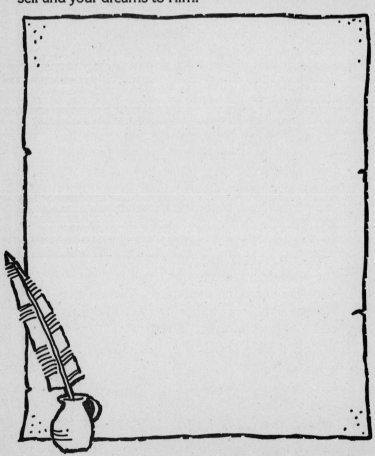

A Closer Look at Commitment

1. Identification

"Yes, I'm a _____. I'm a card-carrying member of this organization."

This is the lowest level of commitment and demands very little. It does, however, offer some security and a sense of belonging.

2. Discipline

"Since I'm a _____, I am willing to alter my life-style to conform to their principles. I attend committee meetings and obey the bylaws, etc."

This is the next level and often requires rescheduling of our weekly activities and our leisure time as well as rearranging of our finances.

3. Enthusiasm

"I'm so convinced that being a _____ is the most fulfilling and satisfactory part of my life, that I willingly go out and recruit others. Besides, most of my recruits are quite willing because they like what they see in my life-style "

It is this level of commitment that will make your ministry most effective. May this be a part of your daily prayer for yourself and those women around you.

Let's close in prayer.

Heavenly Father,

We've just spent a great deal of time analyzing the soil in our churches and we've learned so much. And although we've discovered that some of our efforts are really ministry pitfalls, we are excited about the goals and programs we have outlined. We fervently pray that they are glorifying to you and that they fit into your plans for us. Please bless our continual attempts to understand the women's needs around us by providing us with the energy and desire to get acquainted when needed, to listen with sensitive ears, to read the local papers with a critical eye, and to write across our hearts the mandates included in your Word. May we stop being prisoners of war and be able-bodied planters, instead. In your name we pray and praise.
Amen.

As the rain and the snow
come down from heaven,
and do not return to it
without watering the earth
and making it bud and flourish,
so that it yields seed for the sower
and bread for the eater,
so is my word that goes out from
my mouth:
It will not return to me empty,
but will accomplish what I desire
and achieve the purpose for
which I sent it.

You will go out in joy
and be led forth in peace;
the mountains and hills
will burst into song before you,
and all the trees of the field
will clap their hands.

Instead of the thornbush will grow
the pine tree,
and instead of briers the myrtle
will grow.
This will be for the LORD's renown,
for an everlasting sign,
which will not be destroyed.

(Isa. 55:10-13, NIV)

3
As the Twig
Is Bent

The list of needs you have made in chapter two is notable, I'm sure. I've compiled a list of my own and I'd like to share mine with you:

Spiritual growth
Physical exercise and diet control
Single parenting
Substance abuse
Homosexuality
Financial planning
Death and dying—hospice
Moral concerns
Child evangelism
Latch-key children
Outreach
Developing deep friendships
Missions
Education
Upgrading homemaking skills.

We've been able to compile our lists by becoming more personally acquainted with the women around us. We've also looked more closely at our communities and the needs which might never have come to the attention of our women's groups. Best of all, the desire for a more effective ministry has begun to germinate, take root and even show its spindly shoots above the ground of the status quo!

Ever-Changing Needs

The word "change" occurs with great frequency in our society. And although it may not be a source of comfort to many, it is a consistent reality. It has been estimated that one in five families move every year in America. If this surprises you, consider the number of new neighbors you have seen, the number of friends your children have had to say good-bye to, the number of families who have had to move away from your congregation to follow the demands of career changes. Progress, to many, means change. Movement. The extended family has nearly disappeared and we, as Christian women, must evaluate the needs of those around us periodically. People need us and we must be alert because their needs fluctuate.

What does all of this mean to us and to our lists of needs we have just compiled? It means that our lists are only temporary. Today it is our prayer that they be accurate. Sometime in the future we will pray that some of the needs will have been taken care of so there will be room for the others that will no doubt develop.

Being aware that a list of needs will fluctuate and be full of changes—however unexpected—has been beautifully illustrated to me and a great many others at a Sacramento, California church. It was last year that the pastor's wife (who is also the director of the women's ministry program) became aware of an unprecedented number of pregnant, unmarried women who were coming to the church seeking guidance and support. Knowing well their sensitive and immediate needs, this godly woman knew that God would raise up somebody for them. But who? And how would this woman be found? Believing that the Lord would take care of this need, consistent prayer was started. And sure enough, a retired registered nurse volunteered to enter the lives of these young women to support and love them through their pregnancies. During that year, the need for a pregnancy counselor was so immediate and evident that the women at this Sacramento church added it to their list. And although this particular need has not surfaced since then, others have, and they have been responded to as well.

How often should our lists be reviewed and updated? I encourage you to go through this process once a year. But if needs surface suddenly and unexpectedly, be flexible and move as the Lord calls you. Rejoice when you meet with successes and are able to cross off needs. And lean on the Lord's unending strength when trauma and pain cause others to turn to you with their needs.

Are You Ready?

ALL growth produces change—change which is usually intimidating and always complicating. Take, for example, a Sunday School class that starts the year with four kids and grows to 10 in two short months! This is quite a blessing, but the children must be accommodated. Six more birthdays must now be remembered and more parents communicated with. This also means more prep time and additional follow-up. When you pray for growth, remember to pray that you will gratefully accept the changes.

Ever-Threatening Change

But as the winds of change begin to blow on your seedling ministry, do some of these questions or comments surface?

- "Sometimes we can't seem to get started. Other times we are off in a thousand uncoordinated directions."

- "The right hand of our ministry doesn't know what the left hand is doing."

- "Our present women's organization is afraid of too much change. But some of us feel we need to branch out."

- "There's so much tradition and annual programming that we don't have the time or the energy for any additional ministry opportunities. We have all we can do to keep *this* going!"

- "We're just beginning and really want to meet needs. But we're concerned about becoming too fragmented to staff our various ministries."

NOW is the time to organize our ministries to meet the needs we've worked so diligently to identify. In this chapter I'd like to introduce to you an organizational plan that you will be able to apply—no matter what denomination or church structure you are a part of. But before we move on to this next step, I encourage you to look back at the third comment recorded above. Keep-

ing in mind these women who consider even an evaluation a threat, I offer you now an invaluable lesson in tact.
Your added sensitivity will enable growth without the
degree of pain or tension that might otherwise be
present.

> Are you:
> —the newly *appointed* director of women's minis-
>   tries?
>
> —the newly *hired* director?
>
> —the current chairwoman of the existing women's
>   organization?
>
> —a newcomer who would like to see some ideas
>   that have worked in other churches implemented
>   here?
>
> —available for involvement and leadership for the
>   first time?

Whatever your point of reference, please approach and
include representatives from current ministries in your
discussion. Their inclusion is essential in discussions
involving reorganization ideas or even additional ministries. You need their help and support, and your willingness to move with tact will be honored by the Lord.

I really can't say this strongly enough. Go first to your
pastor for confirmation. Next, approach the organized
women's association already in service and begin your
remarks with an affirmation. "I have an idea and I'd like
your help and support. I certainly can't do it without you
and this becomes especially evident to me when I see

how beautifully you have supported our missionaries throughout the years." This particular comment may not accurately portray your situation, but the essence of the compliment does. Affirming existing services opens the door to new ideas. And although rolling bandages for the missions committee may not be your calling, drug counseling may not be theirs, either. But neither project should be ignored because of the fear of change. Let's tactfully suggest new ideas and see what incredible avenues the Lord will open up to us.

A Ministry Hint

Very few of us are able to motivate ourselves simply because "the job has to be done." Women are motivated best when they feel useful and when their accomplishments are appreciated. Take the time to acknowledge the hard work going on around you by keeping an appreciation bulletin board up-to-date, giving public praise reports, having a yearly appreciation dinner, sending thank-you notes and celebrating with a women's ministry fair. The investments of time, money, strengths, energy and gifts are invaluable. Thank the Lord and your volunteers.

Common Organizational Plans

Within most churches, regardless of size, there are activities or ministries. The Women's Society, the Mothers' Day Out Program, Bible studies and circles meetings are all quite familiar to you, I'm sure. I'm also positive that these programs—and others like them—are very much appreciated by those who are participating. What happens, however, when individual women become aware of what they might consider "pressing needs"? I often see four responses. Do these look familiar?

1. Someone decides to collect a group of women together to meet the need.
2. Someone forms a group of allies and pays a visit to the pastor. They put the ball in his court.
3. Someone decides to verbalize about the lack of action. This is sometimes called complaining!
4. Paralysis occurs because of ignorance and the inability to form a plan of action.

Weak coordination not only eliminates necessary action, but it allows the same old programs to continue year after year—regardless of their effectiveness. A workable organizational plan—a design for a church-wide women's ministry program—is the answer. But over the years, I have been continually frustrated with the typical patterns that are most often suggested. I'm sure you've seen them.

The Wheel

Using this plan, the hub is the director of women's ministries and the spokes represent the various ministries.

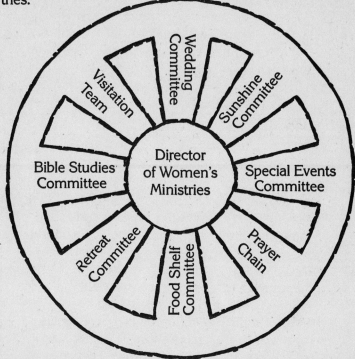

The disadvantages of this organizational plan cause great stress on the participants. Burnout is common.

1. There are too many women responsible to the director.
2. Committee meetings and report sessions are consumed with information that is not necessarily essential to the entire group. For example, those women who are

responsible for the prayer chain will not find it necessary to know every triumph and tribulation experienced by the Food Shelf Committee.

3. The director will find it increasingly difficult to assemble all of the committee heads for regular leadership meetings. They are extremely active with their groups.

4. The director will also find it nearly impossible to relay information to absentees— even if there were minutes taken.

Attitude Check

It was a chilly fall day and I had been asked to speak to a Christian women's gathering. This was their outreach and evangelism luncheon and I was to be a part of their program. But much to my dismay, it became immediately apparent that the chairwoman had managed to recruit her special friends and relatives to help her with the afternoon. The definite "in-group" feeling surfaced immediately as side comments and little personal jokes were sprinkled between the casually introduced guests.

Dear servant, guard carefully against this kind of situation. Show the women of your community how much you care about them and how glad you are that they are a part of your program. The Lord will bless your attitude and great things will be born.

The Traditional Organizational Chart

This is the most common of the charts and is adapted from the organizational charts most often used by businesses.

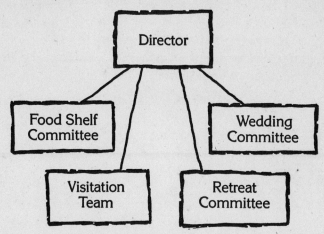

I see three major disadvantages to this organizational plan:

1. Again, the director carries the majority of the responsibilities. Everything stops on her desk.

2. Many of the women feel boxed in and confined to their job descriptions. Territories seem to be drawn and a lack of shared responsibilities breaks down the feeling of sisterhood so many women treasure.

3. Vitality and energy is missing. The flow of activity moves down rather than up the chart.

Growing a Minis-Tree

I've always loved trees and spent many years gazing at them in great appreciation before the Lord showed me how beautifully they can serve us in organizing our entire women's ministry programs. As you look at this simple line drawing of a tree, allow me to explain what the various parts represent and how you can use this model to organize your church-wide efforts.

The Roots

This part of the tree serves as the **authority** for your ministry. And although I see groups who at times are tempted to skip this part of the model, you can well imagine what will happen to your tree without roots! The least little wind of criticism and the tree (your ministry) will topple. Strongly emphasized, women who move away from authority are not blessed in ministry.

Examples of authority can include the Bible, Board of Elders, Deacons, a pastor or a Board of Directors specifically made up of women to oversee the women's ministry program. Name the roots in your church:

The Trunk

This part of the tree represents the **administration** for your ministry. Here is the place for the officers or volunteers. Please be aware that the names you choose are completely arbitrary—although titles can carry various connotations. You may have a president, chairwoman, supervisor, director or administrator. I particularly like the title coordinator because it is less threatening. Other officers that you may wish to include here are a vice-president, secretary, treasurer, publicity coordinator, etc. Name the administrators of your women's ministry here:

The Branches

The branches represent the **areas** of your ministry. But be careful here! These areas should be quite general, so don't be tempted to place your specific programs in this location. Also keep in mind that your areas of ministry should be interdependent.

Most women find this part of the tree the most challenging to classify, so let's go through a helpful exercise that will clear up any questions you may have at this point.

1. List every present activity the women in your church are participating in.
2. Place each activity under a broad category. These may include education, outreach, spiritual growth, etc. Here are some examples:

Education	Outreach	Spiritual Growth
Library	Life with Spice	Bible studies
Moral Concerns Committee	Hello Neighbor Program	Prayer Pyramid

Name the branches of your Minis-Tree here:

The Twigs

The twigs represent the **activities** of your ministry. And unlike the branches, the twigs can be completely unrelated and pruned when interest lags or when a need has been met. Pruning twigs will never kill an entire ministry program—most always it is a "treemendous" growth aid.

I am often asked about those activities that don't seem to fit anywhere—those activities that are not coordinated into the official women's ministry program. Good examples are the wedding and baby showers that are often sponsored by whoever wants to put them on. By taking more time with these kinds of activities and deliberately placing them into a specific area, they become more significant and the women can see the important part they play. Where do you suppose we could put showers on a tree? I see some wonderful results to these activities and this kind of revelation will help us find a logical branch.

1. A wedding shower, sponsored by the women of the church, often includes the bride's friends and relatives who may never have visited the church or been a part of a church family. Seeing the love and concern the church women have for their loved one will appeal to them. They may even be interested enough to investigate the church for themselves.

2. Baby showers often encourage parents to get their children into nursery programs, Sunday School activities and choirs. Seeing how lovingly the adults work with children and value them will speak in a special way to the shower honorees.

Because showers seem to be helping the spiritual life of the participants, I think I would place this activity on the spiritual life branch. I've seen other churches place showers on the outreach branch. The possibilities are endless, as you can see!

List your activities here:

Drawing Your Own Minis-Tree

Now that you have classified the various parts of the Minis-Tree and recorded the information above, turn back to the tree I've provided for you and design your own. Don't feel obligated to fill in every branch. I simply wanted to offer enough branches! Also, take pride in the kind of programs you see! It's exciting and you are God's faithful servant—going out on a limb for Him!

Incorporating Your List of Needs

Referring to the list of needs you have assembled, consider in which area of your Minis-Tree these needs might be met.

Needs	*Branch*

Remember, it is possible to have several kinds of needs met at the same time or with the same program or event. It is most important that your ministry be continually growing and meeting expressed needs.

Advantages of the Minis-Tree

Now that you have had the opportunity to work with this organizational model, be encouraged by this list of advantages:

1. It is a live image
2. It has unlimited growth potential
3. It is designed to produce desired fruit

4. The branches are interdependent
5. It is easily understood
6. It provides a place of refreshment
7. It grows upward, taking the major responsibility off the director
8. It has a stable root system
9. It is extremely versatile
10. It allows for pruning (see John 15) without in any way damaging the other branches. In fact, cutting back in one area allows for greater strength and usefulness in other areas.

Let's dedicate our new Minis-Tree with a prayer.

Precious Lord,
How wonderful it is that we can gaze at the beautiful trees around us and take that lovely vision into our churches. May we be continually open to change and sensitive to those who find it intimidating. May we also aim in every endeavor to work interdependently with those around us when serving you. Your love is overwhelming and your blessings incomparable. May we be grateful servants.

Bless our Minis-Trees, Lord, and bless those women around us who need you so desperately. In your holy name we pray.
Amen.

Reach Up and Reach Out!

*But blessed is the man who
trusts in the LORD,
whose confidence is
in him.
He will be like a tree
planted by the water
that sends out its roots
by the stream.
It does not fear when
heat comes;
its leaves are always
green.
It has no worries in a
year of drought
and never fails to bear
fruit.*

(Jer. 17:7-8, NIV)

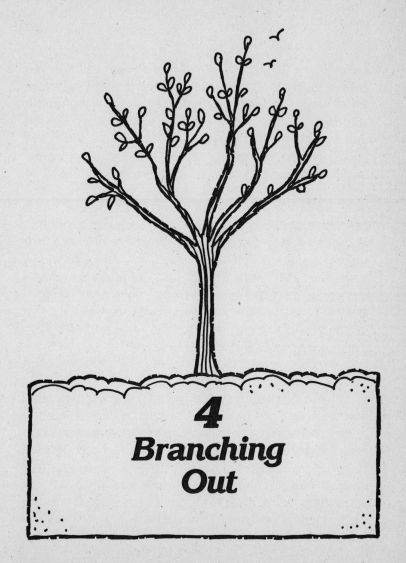

4
Branching Out

One lovely Tuesday morning I received a call from an enthusiastic but somewhat frustrated pastor's wife. She was actively involved in the women's ministry program at their small church of about 200, and although she felt that they were meeting *some* needs, their program was full of inconsistencies—or rather their participants were. Some of the leaders seemed quite organized. They had productive and enjoyable meetings and their activities were top-notch. The women seemed fulfilled and had a real sense of direction. Other leaders felt less in control. Sometimes they did not make good use of their committee members and their meetings were often long and drawn out. Those Branch Leaders who were experiencing success didn't seem to be able to provide concrete help to those who were struggling. "How do you describe what just comes naturally?" one woman asked. This lovely pastor's wife also wondered if maybe there was some competition going on. "We simply need some invigoration," she said.

On the day we agreed to meet I perked some coffee and we spent the next hour or two defining the challenges facing a number of the program volunteers. We also designed a Minis-Tree for her church and decided to focus in on the Hospitality Committee as our test case. It was exciting to anticipate that once we got something down in writing, the expertise of the entire women's ministry program would rise. Immediately she could see the number of burnouts lower and a real sense of harmony develop among everyone in the ministry. We spent the rest of our time together developing some job descriptions, designing a reporting worksheet and outlining some helpful ideas for chairing a meeting.

The most exciting aspect of all of these guidelines is their versatile nature. Not only can coordinators follow these steps when working with Branch Leaders, but Branch Leaders can incorporate these ideas when working with their Twig Leaders!

A Ministry Hint

Somehow we've gotten the idea that a Bible study activity is the catchall. So your neighbor is hurting about her daughter's abortion? Have her attend. You have recently experienced a mid-life crisis and you share your frustrations with a church friend. "Come to my Bible study. It'll really help."

The Bible does, of course, meet our needs in every way. But the activity *name* lacks the support, love and encouragement possibilities a *fellowship* activity naturally has. Avoid culture shock and invite your neighbors to a fellowship. They may very well get the opportunity to experience a Bible study at the activity, but the name will not turn them or you away from the start.

Job Descriptions

There are three typical approaches to providing job descriptions:

1. Some churches choose not to use a job description at all, preferring instead that the women work within their own capabilities. I see this approach as risky for two reasons. First, some women are naturally more capable or have had past experiences that prepare them in a better way. Second, there is a sudden lack of continuity should the position be vacated. What kind of guidelines are there for the new volunteer?

2. Other churches ask the person who has assumed the responsibility to write their own job description as the ministry unfolds. If this system is initiated, it is necessary that some kind of diary or log be kept, recording each activity and the things learned.

3. Most successful churches I've observed choose to write a description that is delineated but still open to individual creativity. It is this third approach that I suggested to my new friend and now to you. I'd like to stress, however, that this kind of job description must be designed and initiated at the church level. Although I am going to share with you the job descriptions we prepared for her church's Hospitality Committee, please be aware that these descriptions may not fit your needs. It is for this reason that I have chosen not to provide you with an entire book of job descriptions. Please note the reasons why we chose certain responsibilities, then pick and choose according to your organization. In other words, be creative! Be versatile! Have fun and dream!

Immediately before we wrote up the job descriptions, we designed a Minis-Tree to reflect the makeup of the committee. Again note how versatile this organizational plan is and how helpful it is to most of us that we have something to visualize:

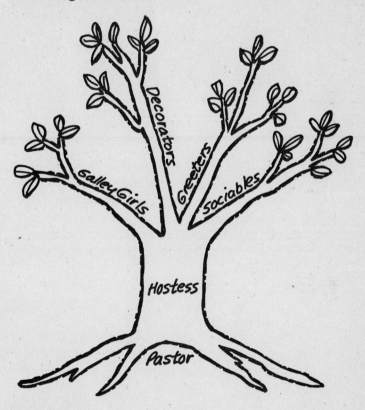

The Hostess

Confident that the Lord has sent along just the right Hostess to head the Hospitality Committee, this is her job simply stated:

1. She will recruit a Head Galley Girl, Decorator, Greeter and Head Sociable.
2. She will obtain the church activities calendar from the pastor—as far as he can give it to her!
3. She will convene a meeting for which she has prepared:
   a. *A beautiful setting* with scrumptious but simple refreshments.
   b. *A short time of devotions and prayer.* She should feel free to ask someone to be personally in charge of this time, reminding them to keep it under 15 minutes.
   c. *An agenda* for the meeting that includes essential enclosures: copies of the church calendar, job descriptions for each committee member, names and addresses of each committee member and a time schedule that she adheres to!
   d. *Name tags* if committee members do not know each other.
4. She will present each member of the committee with a worksheet for the next event. They will fill in the blanks and exchange ideas. The Group Heads will then take the plans to their separate meetings.
5. She will assemble a roster of all Hospitality Committee members and willing helpers. This should be duplicated for everyone's benefit and accountability. Addresses and phone numbers are included.

6. As events are planned, copies of those plans should be given to the pastor for his approval. The worksheets can be used here.
7. She will expect each Group Head to report consistently to her—during each meeting and even between meetings—for communication's sake!
8. She will encourage each Group Head to recruit many others. The goal is for everyone to have a job and to do it excellently.

Head Greeter

She has been chosen by the Hostess and has accepted the following responsibilities:

1. She will attend the Hospitality Committee meetings. There she will report on how well the Greeters are doing as well as learn the best ways to cooperate with the other Heads when planning an event. Her goal is maximum effectiveness!
2. She will arrange to have at least two Greeters EVERY time the church door opens.

What shall the Greeters do? They shall do all those things that will make everyone anxious to return to the Church family.

a. Smile.
b. Pray ahead of time for those who will come into the church and for their needs.
c. Provide appropriate name tags.

    d. Arrive at least 20 minutes before a scheduled event.

    e. Prepare visitors' packets that include a schedule of the services, a greeting letter from the pastor, a tract and any other enclosures you can think of. What about a brochure about your women's ministry program?

    f. Be on the alert for visitors all the time. But don't forget the regulars. Consider phoning those who are new and those who have been absent. Also remember to introduce Sunday School newcomers to the class and the teacher.

    g. Encourage people to sign the guest book, including their address and phone number.

> So, warmly welcome each other into the church, just as Christ has warmly welcomed you; then God will be glorified.
>
> (Rom. 15:7, TLB)

Head Galley Girl

She has been chosen by the Hostess and has accepted the following responsibilities:

    1. She will attend the Hospitality Committee meetings and report on the activities of the

food services as well as learn about the church events that will need their services. She'll also be open to new ideas.

2. She will help to recruit at least three or four others who have a servant-homemaker's heart.

A Ministry Hint

Rather than asking individuals to replace missing kitchen utensils as a love gift, why not sponsor a church kitchen shower! This can be done by purchasing the needed items, displaying them festively and allowing the women to "buy" them right then and there. Not only will you have just the items you need but the purchasing fund will be reimbursed immediately. Of course, fun and games will be included with this shower along with something delicious to eat and drink!

What will the Galley Girls do? They will do all those things that will make the kitchen and food services of the church a delightful means of joyful fellowship.

a. Pray that the Lord will honor the church kitchen with His presence and sweet spirit—in the lives of the Galley Girls and all who use it.

b. Replace equipment as needed.

c. Take inventory of the kitchen and post where things belong in the kitchen.

d. Write a list of guidelines for the use of the kitchen, posting them creatively and prominently.

e. Post at least two phone numbers to call for clearance to use the kitchen facilities.

> *She watches over the affairs of her household.*   (Prov. 31:27, NIV)

Head Decorator

She has been chosen by the Hostess and has accepted the following responsibilities:

1. She will attend the Hospitality Committee meetings and will report on the progress for beautifying the church. She will also learn about the events and services that will be enhanced by their workmanship!

2. She will recruit several others to lead subcommittees.

Room Decorators will evaluate the Sunday School classrooms, fellowship hall and church foyer, considering how to beautify the areas for special programs.

Sanctuary Servants will decorate the sanctuary appropriately for special seasons and events using flowers, displays, banners, etc.

Special-Event Decorators will decorate tables and various other areas of the church beautifully!

Craftswomen will sew, hang, cut and paint—adding their special touch and skills to the home of God's family.

May the favor of the Lord our God rest upon us. (Ps. 90:17, NIV)

Head Sociable

She has been chosen by the Hostess and has accepted the following responsibilities:

1. She will attend the Hospitality Committee meetings, reporting on their activities and learning of the upcoming events. She will be especially aware of the church calendar.

2. She will recruit five or six others to share the blessing!

What shall the Sociables do? They will arrange for the program for the church events. And depending upon the style and theme, they will arrange for music, a film, guest speaker, games or other entertainment.

> *Love each other with brotherly affection and take delight in honoring each other. Never be lazy in your work but serve the Lord enthusiastically.*
> *(Rom. 12:10-11, TLB)*

A short time ago I heard from this small church and they are doing some mighty works for the Lord! I am thrilled that the concept of preparing job descriptions has been the shot in the arm they needed. They have also found the worksheets extremely helpful. And this introduces our next move to branch out.

The Reporting Worksheet

In order to keep everything organized for all events, I suggest that you use a worksheet similar to the one provided here.

"In Christ . . . each member belongs to
all the others" (Rom. 12:5, *NIV*).

Event _____

Date _____

Time _____

Theme _____

1. Decorations

2. Food Service and Cleanup

3. Greeters and Hostesses

4. Special Events

5. Evaluation and Suggested Improvements

This simple tool serves so many purposes and I've seen it revolutionize ministry programs! To see how it can be best utilized, let's use the Hospitality Committee as an example. For each activity the Hostess will pass one sheet out to every Group Head. The heads will fill in their plans in the appropriate sections and use it as a reminder when organizing their helpers. After the activity is over the evaluation section, located at the bottom of the page, can be completed and the entire sheet stored in a notebook or file folder. Not only can this sheet serve as a substitute to the often troublesome minutes, but the Hostess can take a copy to her meetings with other branch heads or the Coordinator. She can then report, with real accuracy, the details of the activities.

Some churches utilize this form of organization and reporting in many creative ways. The paper can be color-coded to represent a particular month or a particular branch in the Minis-Tree. Art can be added to give the page a little pizzazz! Whatever you do, amend the form to fit your needs and remember that they should only be used as an enhancement. But their value is not to be underestimated. Each woman is now held accountable to her group.

Another gentle reminder belongs here. This informational sheet cannot replace hard work, consistency or an acute awareness of the big picture—the yearly church calendar. Keep these things in mind and the worksheets will serve you well.

Planning for a Successful Meeting

Two of the most common complaints expressed to

me involve meetings. First, most women feel that they are expected to attend too many. Second, most feel that meetings run too long and get off the track too often. I've experienced both and these situations frustrate me, too. Let's eliminate these discouraging occurrences by looking carefully at the structure of the Minis-Tree and then at some helpful suggestions for running a successful and enjoyable meeting.

Meeting with the Coordinator

The Coordinator of Women's Ministries convenes a monthly meeting with her Branch Leaders. She sets the agenda ahead of time and includes several items:

1. Prayer time.

2. Report and evaluation time. This involves each member reporting last month's events. The cover sheets should be utilized at this time.

3. Looking ahead to next month's activities. Each Branch Leader can again utilize the worksheets to report upcoming plans. But remember, worksheets need to be filled in ahead of time! You must be organized!

4. The yearly church calendar should be updated.

Because the Coordinator is organized, she need only meet with Branch Leaders once a month. The agenda is set and the possibility of getting off the track is slim.

A Ministry Hint

There are six signals audiences want to hear, according to Ed Wholmuth:

1. "I will not waste your time."
2. "I know who you are."
3. "I am well organized."
4. "I know my subject."
5. "Here is my most important point."
6. "I am finished."[1]

(Just consider how much your committee members would like to hear these promises as well!)

Meeting with the Branch Leader

Are you ahead of me? Thought so! Now you're thinking like an organized Branch Leader! The agenda and meeting schedule is so versatile and so adequate that you can conduct the same kind of planning session with your Twigs. And using our Hospitality Committee model, the Hostess can use this same format with her Group Heads.

Avoid the Hazards

Be on the alert for those meeting pitfalls that discourage your committee members:

1. Tangents probably rank number one and often occur when a meeting goes from being a report session to a philosophical discussion. They can also occur when one branch is more active than another and the Branch Leader is careful to report every detail. Be sensitive to the fact that tangents bore and intimidate committee members. Learn to guide a discussion and include the more quiet members.

2. A poor location can be terribly distracting. Choose your meeting place with care, aiming for a warm, quiet atmosphere where members can have good eye contact.

Include Special Touches

What makes a meeting memorable? Those special elements that take some planning but are usually a joy even for the leader:

1. Please the eye by providing an attractive centerpiece or nice tablecloth.

2. Cover your time together in prayer.

3. Always be prepared ahead of time. Do your photocopying the day before.

4. Include items of interest to committee members. Examples include photos of recent activities, letters of appreciation, newsletter ideas, prayer requests, etc.

Advantages You'll Enjoy

Some of the highlights of my Christian experience have occurred during meetings with my sisters in the Lord. The fellowship and friendships are almost never surpassed and the prayers uttered in meetings are often unforgettable. You will experience consistent support systems, fun and personal growth.

For further information on conducting successful meetings, I encourage you to see my book *Look, You're a Leader!* Included in this book are additional helps and organizational ideas.

Let's cover this new information in prayer, shall we?

> Lord Jesus,
> The process of branching out is exciting and we praise you that we can stretch our limited resources to your glory. We ask your special blessing as we prepare our own individual job descriptions and approach our volunteers with these new ideas. May the changes be welcome rather than threatening and may we enjoy afresh the possibilities you hold for our ministries. Be with us now as we look ahead at the ideas you have for us when recruiting and equipping our leaders. It is with praise and in your holy name that we pray.
> Amen.

*I am the true vine, and my Father
is the gardener. He cuts off every
branch in me that bears no fruit,
while every branch that does bear
fruit he prunes so that it will be
even more fruitful. You are
already clean because of the word
I have spoken to you. Remain
in me, and I will remain in you.
No branch can bear fruit by itself;
it must remain in the vine.
Neither can you bear fruit
unless you remain in me.
I am the vine; you are the branches.
If a man remains in me and I in him,
he will bear much fruit;
apart from me you can do nothing . . . .
This is to my Father's glory, that
you bear much fruit, showing
yourselves to be my disciples . . . .
This is my command:
Love each other.
(John 15:1-5,8,17, NIV)*

5
**Out on
a Limb**

As your Minis-Tree takes shape and you look over the diagram, it is very possible that the only new people you will immediately need are the Branch Leaders. As your ministry unfolds and develops, you may need Twig (activity) Leaders. But for now, concentrate on the branches.

The entire process of recruiting leaders is a fascinating one and you will want to call on extra measures of sensitivity and encouragement as you approach women. But we will not simply focus our attention on recruiting, for many women will not agree to taking on added responsibility because they feel unprepared. They feel like unskilled laborers! It is for this reason that I will also share with you some ideas involving *equipping* leaders. And although my book *Look, You're a Leader!* deals with this extensively, and I highly recommend that you use it as a supplement to this chapter, I will include information here that is not available anywhere else in our ministry materials.

Some Secrets to Recruiting

Recruiting from a Biblical Perspective
Turn in your Bible to Exodus 18, a familiar portion of Scripture which tells us about Jethro, Moses' father-in-law. Moses and the people of Israel have been through a great deal already when we come to this passage. They have crossed the Red Sea, having been rescued "from

the hand of the Egyptians" (v. 9). They are on their way
to the Sinai. But before their next move, they are
camped in the desert and it is here that we learn of the
family reunion that takes place between Moses, his wife,
two sons and Jethro. Moses shares with Jethro how the
Lord has been providing for them and both men rejoice.

Now look at verse 14. Moses has been listening carefully to his people and helping to end disputes. But
Jethro says, "What is this you are doing for the people?
Why do you alone sit as judge, while all these people
stand around you from morning till evening?" Moses
replies that he feels he is doing the will of God. (Does
this sound all too familiar? How many women do you
know that are handling activities on their own?)

Jethro's reply is a very important portion of Scripture
as far as the development of a women's ministries pattern. Read on and see why:

What you are doing is not good. You and
these people who come to you will only wear
yourselves out. The work is too heavy for you;
you cannot handle it alone. Listen now to me
and I will give you some advice, and may God
be with you. You must be the people's representative before God and bring their disputes
to him. Teach them the decrees and laws, and
show them the way to live and the duties they
are to perform. But select capable men from
all the people—men who fear God, trustwor-
thy men who hate dishonest gain—and
appoint them as officials over thousands, hundreds, fifties and tens. Have them *serve* as

judges for the people at all times, but have them bring every difficult case to you; the simple cases they can decide themselves. That will make your load lighter, because they will share it with you. If you do this and God so commands, you will be able to stand the strain, and all these people will go home satisfied.

Moses listened to his father-in-law and did everything he said. He *chose* capable men from all Israel and *made* them leaders of the people, officials over thousands, hundreds, fifties and tens. They *served* as judges for the people at all times. The difficult cases they brought to Moses, but the simple ones they decided themselves (vv. 17-26, *NIV*, italics added).

Notice that Moses didn't *ask* the men if they wanted to be judges. He selected them and I like that idea. See if you, the Coordinator, can go to a woman that the Lord has dropped into your mind and say, "I have watched you serve and I think that _____ may be an area in which you can serve Him and the women around you. Won't you come? Let's pray together, trusting that the Lord will make it apparent to you and several others that I am also asking to take on leadership roles." You can then go on to explain that the women's ministry program is being reorganized and Branch Leaders are being recruited to take on specific areas of ministry. That way more of the activities and the women involved in these programs will be receiving a greater share of the personal attention they deserve.

Jethro's Warning. Included in this passage is a warning which I hinted upon earlier: Trying to carry the entire load of a women's ministry program is impossible. What did Jethro say? "The work is too heavy for you; you cannot handle it alone" (v. 18). Let the Minis-Tree work for you and avoid this impossible situation. The only results are extreme discouragement, impatience and irritability.

The Benefits. Jethro's comments are also laced with benefits and I encourage you to get strength from verse 23: "You will be able to stand the strain, and all these people will go home satisfied." You won't have to get mad at Sarah because she dropped the ball. There will be others who can pick up where she left off. The **deep** and spiritual satisfaction of having a place, a purpose and a voice will be felt by every woman involved in the newly-formed ministry program. Successes and "failures" will be shared by the marvelous group of individuals who serve the Lord.

Seven Qualities of Leadership. Take a final look at the qualities of leadership mentioned in the text:

1. A willingness to serve
2. Pure motives
3. A sense of personal holiness
4. A willingness to submit to one another
5. A teachable spirit
6. A willingness to share the burden
7. A willingness to teach and create other leaders.

These are all important and should be kept in mind as you approach women for leadership. Remember that you are only limited by the number and commitment of the women in your church ministry.

Are They Forgotten?

No doubt some women have been serving for years without the sense of having been "grafted into" the general ministry program. You may even be aware of some activities that have been conducted without anyone really being able to define how it has worked all of these years! These are the women you might dare to "go out on a limb for" —even if it simply means encouraging those who have kept the kitchen clean for years without anyone realizing who has done it.

Name some women in your church who have been serving for years without recognition (or without the hope of ever being replaced).

Recruiting with Questionnaires

Some churches I have had the pleasure of speaking to and working with have found success in appealing directly to the women of their church. Although they discovered that a personal follow-up was an essential second step in the process of recruiting women for leadership, a significant number of women rooted their talents in the women's ministry program by this initial step. I'm grateful to a church in northern California for sharing their questionnaire with me and now with you.

You Can Be a Very Important Part of Our Women's Ministries!

Women's programs are planned, scheduled and operated by volunteer women just like you! Will you join in this rewarding and fulfilling service?

Yes! I would like to put my faith into action by serving in the following area(s):

SPIRITUAL GROWTH BRANCH

—24-Hour Prayer Ministry
—Prayer Chain
—Jackie's Bible Study

SERVICE BRANCH

—Ministry to the Elderly
—Blood Bank
—Communion
—Nursery
—Weddings
—Kitchen
—Bereavement Dinners
—Decorating
—Volunteer Office Staff

(Chart continues on next page.)

SPIRITUAL LIFE BRANCH

—Ladies' Monthly Luncheon
—Topical Seminars
—Women's Retreat
—Exercise and Diet Class
—Boutique
—Ball Teams

OUTREACH BRANCH

—Life with Spice
—Compassionate Friends
—Unwed Mothers
—Rape Council
—Visitations
—Jail Ministry
—Physical Abuse

EDUCATION BRANCH   SUGGESTIONS

__Missions
__Library   _____
__Look, You're a Leader!
  (leadership training)   _____
__Moral Concerns
  Committee   _____

                           _____

                           _____

                           _____

__I am willing to serve in leadership. I prefer the
branch:

_____

__I cannot serve on a committee at this time but I am
interested in participating in the areas checked above:

Name _____

Address _____

City _____ Zip _____ Phone _____

_____

Choose Your Leaders

Recently, on Dr. James Dobson's radio program, "Focus on the Family," the incredible Dr. Bob Benson spoke on John 15. He reminded his audience over and over again, using poignant examples from his own life, that we all need to be loved. In verse 9 he read, "As the Father has loved me, so have I loved you" (*NIV*). The Lord Jesus has *chosen* to love us, to reach out and show us that we are the valuable branches. We are connected to our precious Lord by love. He takes us just as we are.

Women of God, how important it is that we approach women in love and let them know, by our words and our actions, that they, too, are chosen. And just as we have the opportunity to bear much fruit on our branches, so can all women in our churches. When you approach individuals with the opportunity of leadership and involvement, remind them that they are deliberately chosen. They are not the second choice or the runner-up—they are the Lord's very own.

Equipping Leaders

On the Education Branch of your Minis-Tree you will want to develop an ongoing plan for equipping and training your leaders. You will be more successful in recruiting leaders if each woman is given some special skills and encouraged in her ministry. James Ulrich, a Christian educational consultant, addresses the entire church ministry when he answers the question, "Why equip church leaders?"

A consequence of failing to equip leaders

is that, in the short run, the status quo is preserved, and problems and shortcomings in the system are perpetuated by default. And in the long run, since leader after leader inherits a position without guidelines for improvement, the programs administered by the leaders become less and less effective.[1]

Mr. Ulrich goes one step further by offering us an excellent list of potential benefits. I give them to you now as an added incentive!

1. Individual leaders are helped to grow, to develop their spiritual gifts, and to use them.
2. Those whom the leaders serve and who participate in programs run by the leaders are edified.
3. The church is able to run more efficiently so that more work for the Lord gets done.
4. The church's commitment to developing leaders encourages more people to volunteer.
5. The saints do the work of the ministry and the Body of Christ is built up (see Eph. 4:12) and God is glorified.[2]

Scripture offers some benefits, too. Look up the following passages and discover some added joy to equipping women for service. Pay particular attention to the Scripture passage in Ephesians. That entire discussion, which encourages us to submit ourselves and to make a present of ourselves to each other, is beautiful.

1. _____(1 Thess. 5:11)
2. _____(Titus 2:3-5)
3. _____(Phil. 2:1-4)
4. _____(Eph. 5:21; Rom. 12)
5. _____(Phil. 2:7)

Added Responsibility

Whether it's learning how to run the copy machine in the church office or getting the necessary license to drive the church van, you will always be given more responsibility and more will be expected of you when you accept the offer to be better equipped. It is precisely for this reason that many women avoid involving themselves in additional learning processes. Be aware of this pitfall when you offer new skills— there is fear and intimidation in the minds of many women.

The Leader-Learner Training System

The simplest, least expensive and one of the most effective forms of training is what I call the "Leader-Learner System." The leader finds a teachable woman to be her co-worker. Don't confuse this with team teaching, which I find to be unwieldy because everyone must always defer to one another or meet for a group vote.

"Shall we have cupcakes and punch?"

"I don't know, it might be too early. What do you think?"

It is far simpler to have the leader-learner relationship so there is not that constant sharing that must go on as in a team. Instead the leader can point out to the learner what she is going to do or give the learner a portion of the responsibility. I've already mentioned some advantages but there are three more that I offer as encouragement:

1. **Accountability.** Someone can pray for the learner, coach and encourage them. The leader can step in should the need arise.
2. **Female companionship.**
3. **A biblical pattern.** Paul and Timothy had this kind of working relationship for a time and we can learn much from them.

Ongoing Leadership Training— Look, You're a Leader!

I recommend to you an extensive look into leadership training by the use of another book of mine entitled *Look, You're a Leader!* This material, made up of a paperback and a resource manual for the leader, is versatile, fun and growth producing! It can be used in a variety of ways including:

- A regular course offered yearly
- A Sunday School series
- A once-a-month evening program
- A weekend leadership retreat
- A seven-week evening series.

Acknowledge Your Gifts

Does the discovering of our gifts naturally precede our finding a place of fruitful, satisfying ministry through our churches? This debate continues and I don't have the answer. I challenge you to think this through as you equip your women for ministry. But what I do know for sure is that each one of us are gifted individuals! We have been given all we need for accomplishing God's will. And in knowing our gifts, we can be placed in our most effective roles.

Incentive. The compelling power of the gospel of Christ and His cross *must be* the incentive for our ministry. He has called us to be agents of the reconciling message of the cross. Read 2 Corinthians 5:18-19.

Inspiration. Christ promised power and God's presence as we serve Him. As we receive the gift of forgiveness, we receive God's spirit. The Holy Spirit then provides power and the desire to serve. Our creativity is a result of His work in our lives. Read Ephesians 3:14-20 and 1 Corinthians 12:4-7.

Information. The magnificent gift of the Word of God must be received, studied and then taught. Women's ministries must include the sharing of the gift of the Word to all within our influence. Read 2 Timothy 3:14-17.

Each of these gifts begin with the letter *I*. Can it be that the Lord Jesus means that *I* should be willing to become part of the gift itself? That *I* should receive it, identify with it and become an intercessor?

Ideals	Information
Ideas	Intercession
Incentive	Involvement
Inspiration	

Discover that every spiritual gift and the power for doing His will are yours, in Christ.

A Moment on Spiritual Gifts

There are numerous and excellent books on the subject of spiritual gifts and I believe that it is essential for you to discover your own and encourage the women in your ministry program to discover theirs, too. *Your Spiritual Gifts Can Help Your Church Grow*, written by C. Peter Wagner and published by Regal Books, is an excellent resource. You also have, without any doubt, books in your church library that will be helpful.

Dr. David Hocking has developed three keys to discovering your gifts and I think this whole process is a real gem. He asks three simple questions:

What gifts would you like to see developed in your life? Read 1 Corinthians 14:1, Psalm 37:4 (this is a special gift of God also spoken of in Phil. 2:13), and 1 Timothy 3:1.

What gifts bring you the most joy in thinking about them and using them? It is kind of fun to be in a group where you hear someone enthusiastically suggest a trip to a nursing home while the others groan at the suggestion. We all have our special gifts and the distinctives are delightful. Read Philippians 2:17-18 and 4:4.

What gifts have you found to be effective in terms of results and in the eyes of other believers? What works for you? It is a remarkable experience to have accomplished something that has also brought you great joy. And how special it is when someone says, "I don't know how you did it but you really whipped that program into shape!" There are lots of ways in which we can confirm the gifts we see in each other. Read 1 Corinthians 12:7 and 14:12; Ephesians 4:12 and Romans 1:11-12.[3]

A Ministry Hint

Not only do the worker bees need care, but your leaders need a constant flow of TLC also! Here are some all-time favorites:

- Begin a prayer support system. You may want to group the Twigs and the Branch Leaders together.
- Remember birthdays, anniversaries and other important dates.
- Put on occasional recognition dinners, allowing the women to bathe in the afterglow of a successful activity. Slides, flowers and gifts of thanks are always a hit!
- Keep a file of greeting cards that can be sent at a moment's notice. The Lord will bring to your mind those who need your special care.

A Whole New Thought on Gifts

I'd like to close this chapter with a thought on spiritual gifts offered by Pastor Darryl Larson. He suggests that perhaps we should reevaluate the way we go about structuring our congregations and appointing people to fill the tasks. He points out that it is most common for a church or ministry to create positions and *then* hunt for people to fill them. "Why not do it the other way around?" he asks. "*Discover* first the gifts for ministry that God has appointed in any given congregation, and then allow those gifts to determine the organizational structure through which the ministry is performed. Through His gifts God has provided the design and the dynamism for doing His work in the world. The rediscovery of that fact can only result in greater glory to God and joy for us."[4]

The challenge is ours.

I can never stop thanking God for all the wonderful gifts he has given you, now that you are Christ's: he has enriched your whole life. He has helped you speak out for him and has given you a full understanding of the truth; what I told you Christ could do for you has happened! Now you have every grace and blessing; every spiritual gift and power for doing his will are yours.   (1 Cor. 1:4-7, TLB)

Our Father,
We have so much to think about when it
comes to the areas of recruiting and
equipping the women in our lives for
service. And we are so grateful for the
wealth of materials available to us now.
Your precious Word and Jesus' promise in
John 15, that we are the branches, created
to bear fruit, is perhaps the most
encouraging thing to us right now. Oh, to
know that you have such high hopes for
us and that you take us just as we are is
almost too much for us to take. But we
do—for you are our great hope.

Bless the women around us—those new
Branch Leaders who may have some
strong fears deep inside. Comfort them and
give them confidence. Forgive the others of
us who are not living lives that are full and
ever expanding. Help us to overcome our
fears and take a great big step toward you.
In your name we pray and praise.
Amen.

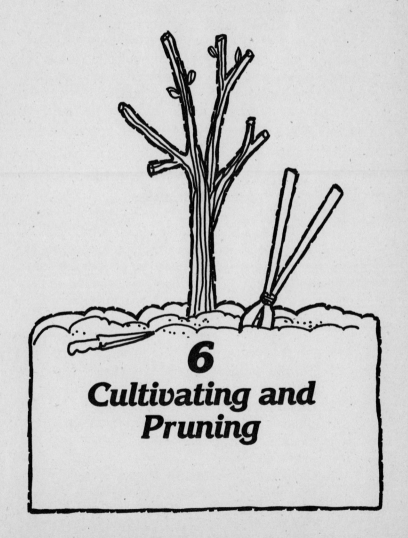

6
Cultivating and
Pruning

It is an exciting and fun process to dream big, create a tree and anticipate its growth. But if the word doesn't get out to your women about the wonderful things their ministry program is doing with and for them, you have missed a vital step in the communication process. Those women who have been recently recruited are eager to get started. Eager, too, are those who are a part of the general church population and *may* be considering their role. Get the good news of your ministry out!

Working with the Church's Yearly Calendar

One of the easiest and most effective methods of working with a yearly church calendar is to incorporate a color coding system. The colors you choose are completely arbitrary, but the Coordinator should insure that each color consistently represent a specific type of program. For example:

1. Black—represents all fixed calendar events like weekly meetings, Bible studies, Mother's Club, prayer groups, holidays, etc.
2. Green—leaders' meeting dates.
3. Blue—all-church events like missions conferences, special seminars, a preaching series, etc.
4. Red—special Women's Ministries events like retreats, district rallies, conferences, etc.
5. Purple—potential or alternative events.

Did you notice my specific mention of the Coordinator? She is the one who handles the calendar at the monthly meeting she holds with her Branch Leaders. Each Branch Leader comes to the monthly meeting with program plans developed by the Twigs. Each Branch leader will, in turn, submit her branch's plans for consideration. If there is space and the group is in favor, the programs are placed on the master calendar.

During any given Branch Leader meeting the following additions to the calendar could be made. The Spiritual Growth Branch Leader comes with several programs she is seeking approval for. She is given the green light by the committee and she adds the activities right then and there. Since the Bible studies are ongoing activities, they are written in using black ink. A future retreat is coded in red. A prayer seminar is marked with blue. This Branch Leader will go back to her group of Twigs and their hard work and planning will continue! Nice to see that there are dates open.

It is at this point that I am often asked a simple but extremely important question: With all of the ideas that are generated by creative, enthusiastic women, how do they ever make definite decisions? I often answer this question by asking another one: How do you make decisions involving your personal schedule?

Making Activity Decisions

For years I have incorporated into my personal life a specific decision-making process. This system is easily adapted to the Minis-Tree.

There are six steps:

1. Set up a three-month calendar. Each of us needs a well-ordered calendar at our fingertips. We need to visualize our commitments. If this process is not a regular part of your life, I highly recommend you purchase Bonnie Wheeler's excellent book, *The Hurrier I Go . . . .* It is published by Regal Books and takes an interesting approach to our use and organization of time by stressing stewardship.

2. Write in on your calendar the known commitments.

3. Evaluate possible areas of ministry by making a list of personal desires, talents and abilities. You may want to consider such activities as leading a Bible study, joining the choir, becoming a den mother, chairing a tea, teaching vacation Bible school, etc.

4. Choose the areas of specific ministry, considering carefully:
   a. The time commitment
   b. The expenses involved
   c. The preparation time needed
   d. How this commitment will affect the others to whom you are already committed.

5. Add new dates of ministry commitment based upon your decision.

6. Cover yourself in earnest prayer.

The Preparation Path

What is a preparation path? It is a road map that keeps a committee on track when planning an event. I had the delightful opportunity of sharing this organizational idea with a California church one summer and you can guess my delight when I saw it put into action the next spring. The Spiritual Living Branch decided to put on an extravaganza they called their "Joyful Living Seminar," and their actual plans I offer to you now.

Step 1: Dream Big

For an activity of this size, the committee members knew they would have to plan thoroughly. But to do this they would first have to dream—then they could respond with action. Take a look at what they envisioned for the event.

Purpose: expose the unchurched to the joy of Christ; reach a cross section of women; enrich personal lives; challenge women to commitment; challenge our members to extensive involvement; reach professional women.

Objectives: 500 in attendance; 250 unchurched; 100 registered commitments; 100 workers involved.

Benefits: promote workshops; introduce our church; have an uplifting women's fellowship; provide an opportunity for ministry; development of people.

Plan: date; 15-20 workshops; have a super luncheon; provide a dynamic speaker; have a general session; have a special feature; sell tickets in pairs.

Budget: honorariums $_____; speaker expenses $_____; workshop expenses $_____; luncheon

$_____x 500; promotion $_____; tickets, inserts, flyers and posters $_____; handouts $_____; decorations $_____; name tags $_____; receipts $_____.

Personnel: Director; Program Coordinator; Promotion Coordinator; Prayer Coordinator; Workshop Coordinator; Hospitality Team Coordinator; Decorations; Kitchen Help Coordinator; Follow-up Coordinator; Ticket Sales Coordinator; Advisors.

Promotion: tickets; inserts/flyers; table hostesses/ticket sales; posters.

Follow-up: table comment cards; follow-up letters; follow-up teams; evaluation sheets.

Schedule:
- 8:30　Registration
- 8:45　Opening session
- 9:00　Music
- 9:15　Speaker
- 10:00　Move to workshop 1
- 10:15　Workshop 1
- 11:00　Move to brunch
- 11:15　Brunch
- 12:00　Music and special event
- 12:15　Speaker
- 12:45　Move to next workshop
- 1:00　Workshop 2
- 1:45　Move to next workshop
- 2:00　Workshop 3
- 2:45　Move to final session
- 3:00　Final session with music
- 3:10　Speaker
- 3:40　Comment cards
- 3:45　Dismiss

Step 2: Job Descriptions

Enthusiasm ran so high after the brainstorming session held at the branch level that volunteers immediately appeared. Women were assigned specific positions and given a job descriptions. (See chapter 4 for my discussion of job descriptions.)

Below you have a summary sheet:

PERSONNEL
Advisors: _____

Ticket Sale Coordinators: _____
                    Design and print tickets; sales

Director: _____
    Delegate responsibility; communicate information; supervise coordinators; look for loose ends; recruit task force; line up program; encourage personnel; re-recruit MC for the brunch; continuing correspondence and thank-yous.

Physical Arrangements: _____
    Material distribution, room setup, audiovisuals; room assignments; room cleanup; custodial liaison.

Promotion Coordinator: _____
    Develop brochures and flyers; recruit table hostesses; posters; skits; news releases.

Prayer Coordinator: _____
    Table hostesses; circle involvement; prayer cards

Workshop Coordinator: _____
    Select leaders with task force; correspondence;

honorariums; thank-yous; determine topics; work with Facility Coordinator; print handouts

Hospitality Team Coordinator: _____
Obtain "freebies"; registration; name tags; packet distribution; information agents.

Decorations Coordinator: _____
Stage; tables; main auditorium; coordinate theme.

Kitchen Help Coordinator: _____
Recruit for setting tables; ask men to serve and clear.

Follow-Up Coordinator: _____
Print and collect comment cards; recruit/train follow-up team; monitor follow-up and report results.

The ability of committee members to communicate, share ideas and hold each other accountable is enhanced by the single-sheet job descriptions. A listing of addresses and phone numbers would be a welcome addition to this form.

Step 3: Determining the Preparation Path

This informational piece is developed by the committee starting from the last event and working backwards. Because this committee decided to have an evaluation meeting (which I highly suggest and would add that it should also be a celebration/thank-you evening complete with slides, gifts, etc.) they began there. The most important actions were placed on the path with corresponding dates. The path was then photocopied and distributed to all members of the committee. The accountability value rings true here, as well.

PREPARATION PATH—WORKSHEET 1

September	Determination of workshop topics
October	Confirm workshop leaders/hotel reservations
November 14	Brochure designed
December 12	Brochure printed
January 2	Promotion begins/prayer strategy begins
January 16	Tickets designed and to printers table hostesses recruited
January 23	Train table hostesses/ticket sales begin
February 13	Recruit men for work details
February 27	Ticket sales/comment cards printed
March 1	Get checks for honorariums/rooms and equipment divided
March 4	Set tables/thank-you letters to workers/ train hospitality women
March 5	THE DAY OF JOY!
March 14	Evaluation meeting

Just a Housewife

Hello, Mrs. Jones? I've just called to say
I'm sorry I cried when you called today.

No, I didn't get angry when your call came at 4
Just as the Cub Scouts burst through the door.
It's just that I had such a really full day
I'd baked 8 pies for the P.T.A.

And washing and ironing and scrubbing
the floor
Were chores I had finished not too long before.

The reason I cried and gave that big yelp
Was not cause you phoned to ask for my help.

The comment that drove me berserk
Was, "I'm sure you'll have time because
YOU DON'T WORK!"

Author Unknown

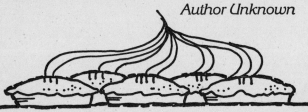

There is another preparation sheet that is most helpful to the individual worker. The information on this sheet pertains specifically to her and becomes a progress report at meetings and a top-notch reminder over the months! This worksheet is a critical second step to organizing a preparation path and a copy is given to the Coordinator. Please note that such a worksheet would need to be greatly expanded for a program as large as the Joy for Living Seminar. As you see it here it is an excellent tool for the Branch Leaders to hand out to the Twigs or the Twigs to their committee members. As always the goal of versatility is met and the information is transmitted painlessly!

PREPARATION PATH—WORKSHEET 2

Committee _____

Chairman _____

(name, address and phone #)

Committee Members: _____   _____

_____   _____

_____   _____

Job Description:

Your own opportunities/responsibilities:

Month/Dates   Goal

The women organized themselves extremely well, left nothing to the last minute and covered all decisions with prayer. As a result their Seminar day was a huge success.

The Fine Art of Communication

All of this planning will certainly prepare an excellent program. But your ministry will never get off the ground or begin to grow up unless you get the word out about the wonderful opportunities available through your church's Women's Ministry Program! There are lots of ways to "reach out and touch someone" and that includes the telephone!

The Tele-Tree

I begin with this method of communication because it is a delightful combination of leasts and bests: it is the least expensive and the least time consuming. It is also the most productive way to communicate with women and you will reach the largest number of women.

Are you a bit skeptical? I encourage you to take an unofficial poll the next time you present a program. Ask various women why they came. I doubt that any significant number will indicate that they came out of personal curiosity or because they saw a notice in the bulletin or on a poster. Although these methods of promotion can be considered successful if even one woman comes because of their prompting, the great majority of your women will attend an activity because of a personal invitation that came their way in one form or another. No doubt a friend called and asked, "You're going, aren't you?" Or someone agreed to meet them in front so they could sit together.

Don't simply challenge your women to bring a friend. Enable your women by using a non-threatening, personal form of contact. Here is how the Tele-Tree works.

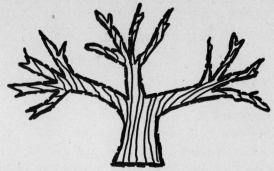

1. Put up a phone chart at your next meeting and ask for volunteers. Those who would like to be a part of this program should then be asked to put their name and phone number on a 3x5-inch card. The Tele-Tree Leader will collect the cards and form the actual tree at home.
2. Point out that each woman will be given a short script and will only be responsible to call four other women when the tree is initiated.

There are several advantages: First, a large number can be contacted in a very short time. Second, nobody is over-burdened by too many phone calls. Third, a script will help those who find phoning a bit intimidating. Fourth, there is far less opportunity for breakdown in the system should you be temporarily unable to reach someone on your list. There is no chain to break.

A final thought to add to your success. It is extremely important that the women selected for the trunk of the Tele-Tree be dependable. A good start will get the word out!

Especially Touched

In their book, which describes how they have coped with a mentally ill son, Jack and Joanne Hinckley make a noteworthy comment regarding personal touches initiated by the phone. After their son John had attempted to assassinate President Reagan, a member of the church they had been sporadically attending called to offer personal and prayer support. Not only was this gesture perfectly timed as the Hinckleys dealt with their pain in extreme isolation, but the outreached hand opened the door to church involvement as they had never before experienced it.

The Printed Page

You will probably discover for yourself that the best means of getting the word out is word of mouth. However, the next best form of communication is the printed page—especially one placed in your church's bulletin.

The best form of written communication is the newsletter—handed out. Get organized, prepare your notices ahead of the scheduled event and hand deliver them during a Women's Ministry gathering.

The second most effective printed page is sent by way of direct mail. This is a risky form of communication because so many women throw out "that junk mail" without ever looking at it. Of course, if you use the other methods and add some posters for good measure, you may prompt some women to be on the lookout. Here are some pointers about bulk mailing:

1. To mail on the reduced bulk rate, you need at least 200 identical pieces of mail.
2. The purchased permit number is printed on the mailing side of your brochure. Permit number, you ask? Yes—and your church probably has such a number.
3. Why not enlist the help of the church secretary who probably already knows about the intricacies of this mailing. (Just don't tell her I sent you!)
4. Labels can be typed on Xerox label sheets (33 labels per page—ask your local stationer for help) and photocopied. Or, ask one of your women to put the names and addresses into her home computer!

Preparing attractive and informative notices. It's not difficult. And you are especially fortunate if there is a copy machine at your church. You will find that this form of duplication is best if you have 100 or fewer copies to make. If you have a larger number I suggest you call various quick printers in your community and find the best quote.

Here are some pointers when preparing your notice:

1. Let your imagination be your guide as you collect materials to be duplicated. Pictures from events, a good typewriter and clip art will really add the right touches. I recommend to you the clip art books published by Gospel Light Publications. They are sold

at your local Christian bookstore and include not only fun, attractive and eye-catching art that you literally cut out of the books, but instructions to aid in your preparation.

2. Prepare your master using clear black and white materials. They always produce better.

Tell me—I'll forget.
Show me—I may remember.
Involve me—and I'll understand.

A Women's Ministries Fair

Why not get your new Women's Ministry program off the ground by sponsoring a fair! You have willing and energetic Branch Leaders and the possibilities of fun, more volunteers and giving God the glory are at hand. A few simple steps need to be taken and you are on your way.

1. Enlist the cooperation of a small group of leaders (Branch Leaders would be great). Meet together, pray and support each other.

2. Plan your fair and use the worksheets provided here in this chapter.

3. Let your imagination go as you plan the schedule of events. Remember that this is a celebration, so ensure that many are involved, the colors bright, music upbeat and message clear: It's a joy serving the Lord in a ministry program!

THE HEART-TO-HEART WOMEN'S MINISTRY FAIR

Date: First Saturday in February

Place: Church Fellowship Hall

Decorations: Red and white tablecloths, hearts, ribbon, flowers, lunch boxes, prizes.

Schedule: 9:30—Registration and coffee. Hostesses greet the women with heart name tags and freshly baked muffins with red bows.

10:00—Music and prayer.

10:20-11:20—Speaker.

11:20-noon—Each Branch Leader has seven minutes to explain the ministry opportunities on her branch. Around the room are booths, cleverly introducing the branches. The women are encouraged to visit the booths during the lunch break and register to be involved—for service and growth.

Noon-1:15—The women on the food committee have prepared scrumptious box lunches. Guests are served one-half a Pita pocket sandwich, fruit salad cup, brownie and a mint. The meal is served in a corsage box, tied with red net, heart napkin attached and tiny heart pin cushion attached on top. Each box contains two lunches and the partners are found by matching the half a heart attached to your name tag.

1:15-1:30—Music and prizes awarded to those women who have worked so diligently to put on this fair. A marvelous idea is to award small heart pillows (plans included in this book).

1:30-3:30—Speaker talks about ways women can serve their Lord.

3:30-3:45—Closing remarks.

The Pass It On Heart Pillow

The Pass It On Pillow can be given to family members and friends. Show your love with a kind deed—then lay the heart nearby.
Directions:

1. Use 2-strand thread. Work the words in black and the heart in red.
2. The cross-stitch is cut from a circle and appliqued onto a larger heart, perhaps on red and white checked gingham.
3. Add eyelet trim and red ribbon to complete.
4. Sew and stuff.
5. Note that a 22-count fabric makes a 3x3-inch design. Allow a bit larger piece of fabric for the edge.

I did this
because
I ♡ you

A Ministry Hint

Why not ask your pastor to dedicate your new ministry? At the close of your fair, ask him to come and pray a prayer of dedication. Then you can surprise him with a small sapling tree that can be planted somewhere on the church property. Just watch your Minis-Tree grow!

Listen and hear my voice;
pay attention and hear what I say.
When a farmer plows for planting,
does he plow continually?
Does he keep on breaking up and
harrowing the soil?
When he has leveled the surface,
does he not sow caraway and
scatter cummin?
Does he not plant wheat in its place,
barley in its plot,
and spelt in its field?
His God instructs him
and teaches him the right way.
All this ... comes from
the LORD Almighty,
wonderful in counsel and
magnificent in wisdom.

(Isa. 28:23-26, 29, NIV)

7

*Expecting
a Harvest*

I have a dream . . . . " That speech, given of course by Martin Luther King, Jr., still reverberates over the years since he lifted the eyes and hearts of his listeners from the problems around them. He gave them hopeful imaginings of what they could become—and do!

Let's give way to some dreams of our own, dreams of a more effective, vitally productive and growing ministry for women.

Do you dream of meeting the deepest needs of women and their families—

—who are victims of child abuse, incest or are themselves child abusers? (Three in 10 American homes will be touched by incest this decade!)

—whose homes and marriages are shaky?

—who are alcoholics or are living with alcoholics?

—who have a loved one who has declared himself/herself homosexual?

—whose children are rebellious, on drugs or living with a member of the opposite sex without the commitment of marriage?

—who are on welfare or have tried to keep a family together through an economic recession?

—who carry guilt because of their own inadequacy in coping with stress?

—who are worried because they haven't had any "trouble" lately?

—who have spent years in Bible studies but lack the know-how or sometimes the desire to apply their knowledge to good works?

How can these needs be met through your women's ministry?

It is my hope that this chapter will prompt some

dreams of your own, causing you and your women to focus on workable, realistic programs that can be placed on the various branches of your Minis-Tree. Consider carefully your tree design, adding any of these program ideas that you think will meet needs. You may want to add these ideas using a colored pencil or create a separate tree—labeling it the dream tree!

Picture yourself waking up, delighted with your dreams.

At last! The Women's Ministry is about to blossom. But you have to contend with some specific temptations before your dream can become a reality . . .

1. The temptation to simply invite inspirational speakers to address your group (and believe that the large crowd means you have a large ministry).
2. The terrible temptation to be SO ENTHUSIASTIC that you run right over everyone else!
3. The temptation to think that sponsoring a "worthy project" is all the dream you need!
4. The temptation to believe that you can do it all by yourself.

HAVING REALIZED THOSE TEMPTATIONS . . .

Let's get on with it, enlisting the help and support of ALL women. Reach out and touch someone—preferably with gentleness!

Initiate Progressive Thinking

During this dream process, please beware of the Numbers Game. You've played it, I'm sure. But maybe you were unaware. You become a participant the moment you label an activity "less than successful" or even a "failure" when a great number are not in attendance. Regardless of the size of our churches, we must all guard against our natural response to be disturbed at a low turnout.

Our population is diversifying more and more as the years go by. Working women, for example, will no doubt be interested in many church programs but will be limited in their ability to attend. You, therefore, will need to respond by providing activities that occur in the evening or on the weekends. An exercise class, for working women, may only serve six or seven in any given evening, but it should in no way be labeled a failure. There are probably only that number interested in exercising at that hour! If this particular group of women are having a need met, you are serving the Lord in the very best way. So be on the lookout and initiate some progressive thinking as you consider the program ideas.

Beware!

There are seven easy steps to stagnation. May the Women's Ministry dreamer beware!

1. "We've never done it that way."
2. "We're not ready for that yet."
3. "We're doing alright without it."
4. "We tried it once but it didn't work out."
5. "It costs too much."
6. "That's not our responsibility."
7. "It won't work!"[1]

Ministering Through the Educational Branch

1. Create a Concerns Committee
   a. Alert your women to the ways they can make a difference in our society.
   b. Give accurate information for effecting change.
   c. Process major concerns and offer steps to fighting the problem.
   d. I suggest you see the chapter on soldiering in *Look, You're a Leader!* Specific directions are presented.

To the Management:

I wish you to know that I have joined with others who share my values in a pledge to end our patronage of businesses who market what we consider sexually offensive materials. We ask the support of your management in this effort to improve the moral standards of our community through your merchandising policies.

The card above was prepared by the Concerns Committee at Hope Presbyterian Church in Minneapolis. It was distributed by concerned people whenever they encountered pornography. Why not reproduce it and do the same?

2. Upgrade Your Church Library
   a. Have a library shower. In conjunction with another meeting, provide books that have been loaned on consignment from a Christian bookstore. Allow the women to purchase a book for the library and have the donor's name inscribed on the flyleaf. The sky's the limit!
   b. Include book reviews and library highlights in your newsletter or church bulletin.
   c. Have the library open before and after your women's gatherings. Or, put a library cart in the meeting room and encourage the women to browse during the coffee break.

3. Sponsor various educational classes covering such topics as managing stress, time stewardship, working with the handicapped, home economy, etc.

4. Sponsor ongoing leadership training, using *Look, You're a Leader!* of course!

Ministering Through the Spiritual Life Branch

1. Plan a Retreat
   a. Ask everyone to bring a sleeping bag to the church and join in on the slumber party.

   b. Plan a mini-retreat beginning with breakfast at church or at someone's home. The day will end at 4:00. These special retreats are inexpensive and require minimal planning but can become a very special event! Especially good on the weekends for working women. Call it a Real Treat!

2. Create a Wedding Committee
   a. This committee is led by the Wedding Coordinator who assists the couple, suggests decorations, cooperates with the church kitchen, etc.

   b. This committee can also coordinate the sponsorship of all wedding and baby showers. The wonderful outreach value was mentioned earlier in the book.

3. **Create a Devotional Booklet**
   Have each woman submit one page to a booklet that you compile for a special season of the year. Each page can include Scripture, prayer pointers and a few paragraphs that will make that verse come alive. A nicely designed cover will complete the booklet, which can be sold for a minimal charge or presented to your women as a special gift.

4. **Hold a Breakfast Series for Working Women**
   a. January—A New Year's Prayer Breakfast
   b. April—An Easter Brunch
   c. September—A Hiking Breakfast (cookout)
   d. December—An Advent "Bring a Friend" Evangelistic Breakfast

5. **Enjoy Special Music**
   a. Invite a local senior citizens chorus
   b. Build a women's musical group—a trio, double trio, chorale, etc. Let it be a fun elective on this branch.

Ministering Through the Spiritual Growth Branch

1. **Bible Study**
   a. Some suggested helps for Bible studies can be found in *Look, You're a Leader!*
   b. This teaching is imperative, but please be careful that your ministry does not become a spiritual safety zone— a Dead Sea—with no provided outlet for applying and activat-

ing the truth learned. Be on the lookout for those who don't have the desire or the time to get involved in the "less spiritual" programs of transporting children to sports activities, serving in the kitchen, etc. Protect spiritual growth rather than spiritual pride!

2. Christian Aerobics Class
   a. A program outline is available in *Look, You're a Leader!*
   b. Find someone willing to teach the class, invest in a few Christian aerobic albums and look for the benefits!
   c. Write: New Creation Ministries, P.O. Box 18422, Wichita, KS 67218. They have developed a Christian approach to weight control.

3. Growing Old Together
   An increasing number of women in our churches are widows. Do you have a special ministry for them?
   a. Be willing to listen.
   b. Don't be afraid to touch a widow or widower.
   c. Write notes—they are a lifeline.
   d. Offer practical help like mowing the lawn, washing windows, etc.
   e. Invite a widow to dinner and include your children.
   f. Pray!

    g. Don't expect a quick recovery!

    h. Include them in your women's ministry programs, adding some special acts of love and support to help them over the "humps." Widows delight in being involved in the mainstream with other women. Many live away from their children and miss their companionship tremendously.

Ministering Through the Service Branch

> *Then the righteous will answer him, "Lord, when did we see you hungry and feed you, or thirsty and give you something to drink? When did we see you a stranger and invite you in, or needing clothes and clothe you? When did we see you sick or in prison and go to visit you?"*
>
> *The King will reply, "I tell you the truth, whatever you did for one of the least of these brothers of mine, you did for me." (Matt. 25:37-40,NIV)*

1. H.O.M.E.

    Created by the Sunrise Baptist Church in Sacramento, California, H.O.M.E. means HELPING OTHERS MEET EMERGENCIES. Is this a dream of your women's ministry—to really be available when others are in need? This group concentrates on planning meals for people and their families when illness strikes the home. As you become available, you will quickly see the need for child care, transportation, support—even perhaps providing a supportive friend to accompany someone to court. This ministry can be expanded in so many ways.

2. Attic, Cupboard, Closet
   a. Locate a resource location for clothes and food.
   b. Periodically you may want to have a sidewalk or garage sale to clear out your resource corner. The proceeds can go to this Twig. I offer you some helpful guidelines:
      (1) Limit your hours and the number of days.
      (2) Remember the publicity—an ad works best. But also post notices at the market, Laundromat, bakery or dry cleaner.
      (3) Price the items ahead of time, using erasable or detachable price tags.
      (4) Remember to assign a clean-up group and consider donating the leftovers to The Salvation Army.

3. A Prison Ministry
   a. There are numerous agencies that offer you the opportunity to minister in prisons. Consider inviting a representative to speak to your women. Then branch out to meet this need—even via a letter-writing campaign. For more information contact: M-2

SPONSORS, INC., 1260 A Street, Hayward, CA 94541 or call (415) 886-3116.

b. Another excellent contact is International Prison Ministry, P.O. Box 63, Dallas, TX 75221. They have produced an excellent movie entitled, *Honey, Your Momma's in Prison.*

---

20 Do's and Dont's for Visiting a Prison

DO . . .

1. Visit a prisoner somewhere soon. It will do you as much good as it does for him or her.
2. Dress casually. Avoid flashy clothing.
3. Be there early. Sometimes prison security officials need extra time to process your visit.
4. Smile. It's contagious even in prison.
5. Tell the prisoner how good he or she looks. Self-respect is important, especially in prison.
6. Talk about a bright future. The prisoner will probably do very well when released, but is unsure of things right now.
7. Tell the prisoner about Jesus. He/she will be more receptive to your testimony than you might think.
8. Tell the inmate you care. This has special meaning to someone shut off from daily life in society.
9. Tell the prisoner when you will be back to visit again. He/she will look forward to it.
10. Encourage others to visit in prison. Tell them how well it went for you.

DON'T . . .
1. Be afraid. You are not in danger when you visit in prison.
2. Go without making an advance contact with authorities. If you don't make advance arrangements you will probably be turned away.
3. Take a camera or tape recorder. These are not usually allowed inside.
4. Give the prisoner anything unless you check first with the authorities. Contraband may be suspected if you do.
5. Plan to stay more than about one hour unless you have come a long way. Individual conversation wears thin after that time even among people who know each other well.
6. Bring up family problems. If the prisoner wants to talk about them, you can follow the lead.
7. Talk about the criminal's case. Prisoners would probably like to forget it just as you should.
8. Compliment any part of the prison system. This is a fundamental rule because prisoners do not appreciate their incarceration.
9. Forget to pray daily for those you visit. Pray for their salvation.
10. Forget to contribute to a prison ministry. The need is great.[2]

---

4. Special People Ministry
    This ministry is focused on the blind, deaf, physically and mentally handicapped.
    a. Arrange for someone to "sign" your meetings and services.

b. Build ramps and other facilities for their convenience.

c. Make your tape library accessible to your blind members.

d. Purchase some braille books for your library.

e. Write EVER NOW, INC. Director Pauline Lundell keeps a running correspondence with the people who send her their own writing or just letters offering advice and personal thoughts. This Journal of Christian Fellowship with the Handicapped can be requested by writing: EVER NOW, INC. 4701 Flag Avenue North, New Hope, MN 55428.

5. Minister to the Lonely

Organize visitation teams and create love gifts to carry along with you.

My Special Hope

Hello there!
I feel different already
now that you've arrived.
You're special;
you're something to look forward to—
a godsend in the real sense.

All week, you know,
the mornings, they're the same;
routine, lackluster—
I'd almost say lifeless—
"Eat this, take that,
comb your hair, brush your teeth,
get moving, do your exercise,
watch out, don't bother her,
be careful, how's the weather?
When was your stool?
That plant died.
What's that smell in here?"

One after another,
dreary, dead, almost.

But then you come again,
I always know you will.
You're my secret,
my inside sunshine,
my hope, my mystery laughter,
my happy day!

   What ya' smilin' about, Luv?

That's simple, miss.
Maybe you forgot, but *I* didn't.
It's Sunday!
The Lord's special seventh day just for . . .
I'd never survive without Sunday.

That's great, Luv,
now just open your mouth for me,
big and wide.
My, aren't you the smiley one today![3]

Ministering Through
the Outreach Branch

1. Hello Neighbor
   a. This group has also been called the Christian Welcome Wagon!
   b. You can locate newcomers from several sources
      (1) Through visitors' cards in church
      (2) Through word of mouth and neighbors
      (3) From newspapers announcing births, weddings, etc.

2. *Life with Spice*
   These weekly or monthly get-togethers are designed for neighborhood outreach. The program is written by me and published by Regal Books.

3. Neighbor Packet
   a. These can be compiled and left as door hangers when visiting your neighborhood. Because of our transient populations, a neighborhood canvas should be taken annually.
   b. Packet can include a church welcome brochure, Women's Ministry information, list of phone numbers to call if there is help needed, etc.

4. Evangelistic Coffees
   They can be held in homes and are especially effective near Christmas, for everyone likes to visit neighbors during the holidays. These

often provide a springboard for coffees and get-togethers.

5. Elective Outreach Classes

These classes are designed for church women and their guests. Each session runs six weeks and is a manageable time commitment both for the regular church member and the guest who may feel unsure about attending such an activity. The classes are two hours in length and include fellowship, elective activities, a study and special events.

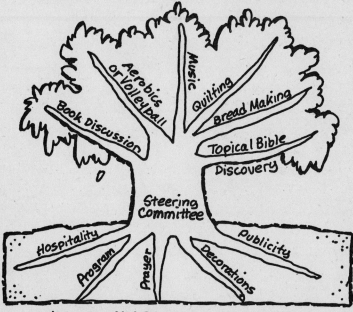

a. Autumn—Mid-September through Early December

Week 1: Special breakfast goodies, elec-

tives explained, sign-ups, committee introduced, study introduced.

Week 2:   9:15 Coffee and welcome
          9:30 Study
          10:15 Electives
          11:10 Closing fellowship
Weeks 3-5: Regular schedule
Week 6: Brunch or cookie exchange

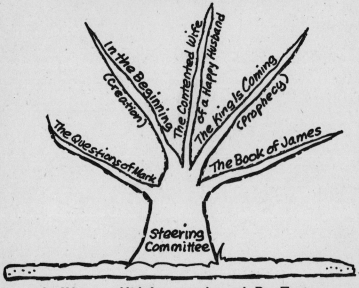

b. Winter—Mid-January through Pre-Easter

Week 1: Special breakfast goodies, elec-
         tives are explained, study intro-
         duced.

Week 2:   9:15 Coffee and welcome
          9:30 Study
          10:15 Electives
          11:10 Closing fellowship

Weeks 3-5: Regular schedule
Week 6: Brunch and show and tell

c. Spring—April and May

    Week 1:   9:15 Welcome and coffee
              9:45 Lecture
              10:20 Discussion
              11:10 Closing fellowship
    Week 2: Meet after the session for lunch at the
             leader's home
    Week 3: Regular day
    Week 4: Outreach Activity—volunteer some-
             where, go door-to-door to greet neigh-
             bors, visit a nursing home, etc.
    Week 5: Regular day
    Week 6: Brunch

d. Summer—June and July

Consider (as we have done in our church
for the last few years) using the *Life with
Spice* idea for a six-week summer series.
This year we will do *Color Me Christian*.
Last year we had a wonderful time with *Be
It Ever So Humble* (visiting biblical
homes). One week we visited Noah and his
family at their houseboat. Our room was
festive with rainbow promise banners and
we ate rainbow sherbet with specially
baked animal cookies and studied our
dependable God in the Word. We even
learned to cross-stitch a bookmark at our
get-together. "It's a Small, Small World"
was our theme when we went home with
Zacchaeus. A dollhouse enthusiast shared
her treasures and we gave a prize to the
shortest woman there! Try it—you'll like it!

Do you notice the progression of these seasonal
trees? First, a simpler study with activity electives. Then,
in winter, there is music and special features with more
intensive small-group studies. In the spring, there is a
study, discussion groups and opportunities for outreach
into the community in practical ways. Each session or
series should conclude with a smashing "Show and Tell"
brunch or luncheon, with the smaller groups each car-
rying part of the responsibility for the special event.

8
Chosen to
Produce Fruit

Time. Seasons. The secrets of living the kind of Christian life God has intended. These are the things I ask you to think about as you look back on the new skills you have learned and as you look ahead to their implementation.

There is a time for planting—a time to know that God's Word is rich and powerful and sharper than any two-edged sword. During this time of planting you open up your heart to the Lord.

There is a time of growing—a time to mature in the Lord.

There's a time for cultivating holy habits—habits that include spending a quiet time in prayer and in the Word daily, attending church regularly and serving.

There's a time for weeding—a time when you pray, "Thank you Holy Spirit for doing your work in my life. The Lord Jesus called it conviction of sin. I'm tired of the devil confusing my life by distracting me from my goals. I choose now to cut out those things that are causing me to miss the mark."

There is a time for pruning—a time full of painful moments when you know that the Lord is doing a mighty work in you. But it's also a time when you can give Him the glory and live life expectantly, waiting for His next wondrous move.

And then there is the time to bear fruit. Jeremiah 17:5-8 (*NIV*, italics added) speaks of the success you will have if you continue to depend on Him:

This is what the LORD says:
  Cursed is the one who trusts in man,
  who depends on flesh for his strength
  and whose heart turns away from the LORD.
  He will be like a bush in the wastelands;
  he will not see prosperity when it comes.
  He will dwell in the parched places of the
  desert, in a salt land where no one lives.

  But blessed is the man who trusts in the LORD,
  whose confidence is in him.
  He will be like a tree planted by the water
  that sends out its roots by the stream.
  It does not fear when heat comes;
  its leaves are always green.
  It has no worries in a year of drought
  and never fails to bear fruit.

The Lord's same words are echoed in John 15:1-8. Turn to this passage in your Bible and read again of the reasons why you are to bear fruit and the glorious results. You will appear as His disciple. You will give the Father glory. You will bear His fruit—IF you remain in Him! But there is more, isn't there. Look at verse 16: "You did not choose me, but I chose you to go and bear fruit—fruit that will last. Then the Father will give you whatever you ask in my name." This is not a blank check to go out and buy that new car you've been wanting! He says that as you live and abide in Him, your desires will be His desires. You can count on His constant provision and it will fill your needs and desires completely.

We Are Chosen

Can you imagine what this can do for you and me? Can you envision what such a message *ought* to do for the spirits of the women in your church? WE ARE A CHOSEN GENERATION, A ROYAL PRIESTHOOD (see 1 Pet. 2:9). Why? So we can show the world how God has pulled us out of the darkness and put us into the light. God doesn't need us—He wants us. And just as our Minis-Tree models demonstrate the aliveness and growth of our budding ministries, God wants us to demonstrate the truth to a dark world. We are chosen to live enlightened lives.

We are also chosen so we may have the glorious opportunity to produce fruit in our lives. And this is one of the greatest ways we can show that we are His.

The Fruit

Soul Winning (The Outreach Branch)

> *I do not want you to be unaware, brothers, that I planned many times to come to you (but have been prevented from doing so until now) in order that I might have a harvest among you. (Rom. 1:13, NIV)*

Some call this fruit the gift of evangelism—leading others to Christ—and this is what Paul did so well. You probably know a number of people who do this quite naturally. But most of us might be embarrassed if asked how many people we have led to the Lord. It scares us out of our wits.

Some believe that we must share the *Four Spiritual Laws* or we have simply not done what is expected. But I remind you of the apple tree when its fruit is hanging so beautifully and temptingly on the branches. We don't need an explanation of the vitality of life from within—it shows on the outside. May we so be like that tree. We may not feel gifted in this respect but we must make ourselves available to live vital lives. Let Jesus show on the outside, then watch the Lord work.

Only 10 Percent

It is important to stress here that not every Christian is called to be an evangelist. All are witnesses to Christ, all must be committed to the church's task of evangelism, but only some are evangelists. (See Eph. 4:11.) It is Peter Wagner's belief that only about 10 percent of those in any church have this particular gift.[1] This means that while those 10 percent should be trained and encouraged in this gift, the other 90 percent (with other needed gifts) must resist a nagging sense of guilt that they are not evangelizing as the others are. But that does not relieve us of the responsibility to be witnesses.[2]

Holy Living (The Spiritual Life Branch)

> *When you were employed by sin you owed no duty to righteousness. Yet what sort of harvest did you reap from those things that today you blush to remember? In the long run those things mean one thing only—death. But now that you are employed by God, you owe no duty to sin, and you reap the fruit of being made righteous, while at the end of the road there is life forevermore. (Rom. 6:21-23, Phillips)*

There is a marvelous product from your life when you say, "Lord, I will live a holy life, shunning the wrong and doing the right. I know that you will make a way for me. Forgive me, Lord, for compromise and for my unwillingness to be inconvenienced."

The last statement in the prayer reflects a challenge that you will face as a leader your entire life. Living for Jesus is inconvenient. Living a holy life, according to this world's standards, is inconvenient. And one of the greatest enemies of our soul is our basic commitment to convenience. But the rocky road of holy living is worked out in righteousness. So make holy living your goal and the reward is eternal life—for you and those who choose a similar life-style because of you.

Some time ago I had a very insightful conversation with Vonette Bright, wife of Campus Crusade for Christ president Bill Bright. I asked Vonette what it is that challenges her most in her ministry. She said, "Daisy, the thing that really gets me going is the fact that Christians have made so little impact on our secular society. We gather, we pray, we support missions. But I believe that God is calling us to bear fruit unto righteousness by holy living."

May we never hear the Lord say, "What more could I have done for you?" Let's live and serve in a holy way.

Sharing Our Material Possessions (The Missions Branch)

> *As you Philippians know, in the early days of your acquaintance with the gospel, when I set out from Macedonia, not one church shared with me in the matter of giving and receiving, except you only; for even when I was in Thessalonica, you sent me aid again and again when I was in need. Not that I am looking for a gift, but I am looking for what may be credited to your account. (Phil. 4:15-17, NIV)*

When we help others, that is bearing fruit. And how many ways there are to help, especially from those of us who live in such a wealthy society. But funny, isn't it, that giving away our material goods can be the most painful gift at times. The Lord simply calls us to look around our world and respond when the need arises. A helping gift can do much for the Kingdom.

Good Works (The Service Branch)

> *For this reason, since the day we heard about you, we have not stopped praying for you and asking God to fill you with the knowledge of his will through all spiritual wisdom and understanding. And we pray this in order that you may live a life worthy of the Lord and may please him in every way: **bearing fruit in every good work, growing in the knowledge of God** . (Col. 1:9-10, NIV, boldface added)*

Whether it involves moral issues and working to make a difference or serving within your denomination, you will have moments when you will stop what you're doing and ask yourself, "Am I too busy for this, too? Am I doing too much? I've got to be careful. I've got responsibilities at home that can't be neglected." This may be a valid question. But may I suggest that this is much more a question of time stewardship. I think we are in far greater danger of doing too little. It is time to look into Scripture and see what is involved in basin and towel services. In fact, we need to quit running to seminars and grab our basins and towels, instead. It is always God's will that we do good things, representing Jesus Christ.

Praise and Thanks

We can bear fruit in our choice to praise rather than complain. In fact, the fruit of our lips can be like an offering. When He comes to gather our fruit, may He see that we have willingly given it to Him.

Choice. This is a great deal of what life is comprised of, isn't it? Even though we have been chosen, we had to choose to be chosen! And from then on we have been choosing. We can choose our attitudes. Think carefully about this, dear leader. We can be caught up in envy as we see all of the "successes" other churches are having around us. Or we can be enthusiastic about our growth potential. We can choose gratitude or grief. We can choose stress or serenity. We can choose to pout or to praise.

Christian Character
(The Spiritual Growth Branch)

> *But the fruit of the Spirit is love, joy, peace, patience, kindness, goodness, faithfulness, gentleness and self-control. Against such things there is no law. Those who belong to Christ Jesus have crucified the sinful nature with its passions and desires. Since we live by the Spirit, let us keep in step with the Spirit. (Gal. 5:22-25, NIV)*

When we have been crucified with Christ we will begin to see these nine characteristics. Isn't this a wonderful honor? We have been chosen to reveal the character of God! My dear friend Barbara Johnson is a woman who has made this choice. She has chosen to respond to some of the devastating things that have happened in her life with cheerfulness. She has a wit that doesn't quit. She often laughs, "I don't know who I am and I'm too tired to find out!" Her ministry is geared to families who have a homosexual member. She knows of the pain, firsthand. But she has chosen to produce fruit with a good sense of humor and a devotion to people around her who may have painful moments, too.

Bearing Fruit with Endurance

The other evening I spoke on the phone with a dear friend of mine. She had had a long day at her office and was facing some challenging deadlines. I had just returned from an extensive week of travel and speaking and I, too, felt fatigued. But our schedules were not the main topic of conversation. We both expressed the frustration of not being better able to meet all of the expectations we had placed on ourselves. There were friends who needed encouragement, husbands who needed our undivided attention for at least a moment and numerous other details that had not been tended to in the ways we wanted them handled. We both so wanted to bear fruit—but where was that extra something we needed at that moment? Quickly we agreed that we could not think of anything better than to be serving our Precious Lord just as we were doing. We also agreed that He would give us the endurance and creativity we needed to meet our expectations.

It was exciting for us to move to California in the early 1950s, and when we stepped into the blue Pacific for the first time, it was tingling! And to actually see the cypress trees on the Carmel coastline . . . !

The LONE CYPRESS on the beautiful 17-mile drive through Carmel and Pacific Grove is a landmark, perhaps one of the most photographed trees in our land. The photo print was assigned to me in a writing class in New York (of all places) over 20 years ago. I wrote the essay which follows at that time.

When we moved back to California several years ago, though we lived among the wondrous redwood trees, we often took visitors to Carmel. There the LONE CYPRESS stands, long after I had written the words on endurance. It has survived vandal's attacks and the test of time.

Many of you have walked with the Lord for several decades, you have *endured,* you have *stayed with it,* and now you are in PRIME TIME, and finding God faithful. Walk with Him into ever more effective minis-trees . . . proving yourself a good and faithful servant . . . .

Endurance

I sat by the shore and pondered.
Within my gaze there was so much that spoke of God. The loudest voice seemed to be saying, "These endure." The backdrop of majestic mountains was nonchalant in the fact of the elements.
The sea continued back and forth, in and out, ebb and flow, roar and whish of pungent tingling spray.
The rocks were anchored fast in the dunes.

In the midst, as a testimonial to endurance, leaned the gray cypress trunk. Occasionally the tufted masses of mosslike greenery would nod in the wind. It was as if to acknowledge the presence of a companion along the irregular coastline. It was not alone, though perhaps in the storm the cypress had felt alone.

The wind, accelerating its power as it approached the obstructions on the shore, had played havoc over the years with the seedling. The creeping Pacific had provided a well for the ever-deepening roots of the little tree. Roots had found so deep an anchor that all the forces of nature could not destroy the life within.

Beauty is often found in the most grotesque forms. The cypress had withstood—not without scars.

As I pondered, God reminded me that the One who endured was blessed, for He would receive a crown of life. The cypress had hers already.

I stood, steadfast in the hope that the crown was worthy of my endurance—and faithfulness.

*When all kinds of trials and
temptations crowd into your lives [my
sisters], don't resent them as intruders,
but welcome them as friends! Realize
that they come to test your faith and to
produce in you the quality of
endurance.*

*But let the process go on until that
endurance is fully developed, and you
will find you have become [women] of
mature character with the right sort of
independence. The [woman] who
patiently endures the temptations and
trials that come to [her] is the truly
happy [woman]. For once [her] testing
is complete [she] will receive the
crown of life which the Lord has
promised to all who love him.
(Jas. 1:2, 12, Phillips)*

Notes

Chapter 1

1. From *Time* magazine, December 27, 1982. Used by permission.

Chapter 4

1. Ed Wohlmuth, *The Overnight Guide to Public Speaking* (Philadelphia: Running Press, 1983).

Chapter 5

1. James Ulrich, "Why Equip Church Leaders?" *Equipping Newsletter: A Church Training Advisory Letter,* Vol. 2, No. 2 (1983).
2. Ibid.
3. Spiritual Gifts Manual by David Hocking—published by Calvary Communications, Inc., P.O. Box 10051, Santa Ana, California 92711. Used by permission.
4. Darryl Larson, "All Christians Are Gifted," *Covenant Companion* (January 1982).

Chapter 7

1. Ed Wohlmuth, *The Overnight Guide to Public Speaking* (Philadelphia: Running Press, 1983).
2. Copyright © 1981 by Allen D. Hanson, Box 9, Ottertail, MN 56571. Used by permission.
3. Elisabeth F. Isais, source unknown.

Chapter 8

1. C. Peter Wagner, *Leading Your Church to Growth* (Ventura, CA: Regal Books, 1976), pp. 72-76. Used by permission.
2. Reprinted from *Called and Committed: World-Changing Discipleship,* Harold Shaw Publisher's edition by David Watson by permission of Harold Shaw Publishers. Copyright © 1982 by David Watson.